W9-AKW-620

OLYMPIC
NATIONAL PARK

ADVENTURE EXPLORE DISCOVER

SUSAN JANKOWSKI

MyReportLinks.com Books
an imprint of

 Enslow Publishers, Inc.

Box 398, 40 Industrial Road
Berkeley Heights, NJ 07922
USA

MyReportLinks.com Books, an imprint of Enslow Publishers, Inc. MyReportLinks®
is a registered trademark of Enslow Publishers, Inc.

Library of Congress Cataloging-in-Publication Data
Jankowski, Susan.
  Olympic National Park : adventure, explore, discover / Susan Jankowski.
     p. cm. — (America's national parks)
  Includes bibliographical references and index.
  ISBN-13: 978-1-59845-092-7 (hardcover)
  ISBN-10: 1-59845-092-1 (hardcover)
  1. Olympic National Park (Wash.)—Juvenile literature. I. Title.
  F897.O5J36 2008
  979.7'98—dc22

                              2007017341

Printed in the United States of America

10 9 8 7 6 5 4 3 2 1

To Our Readers:
Through the purchase of this book, you and your library gain access to the Report Links that specifically back up this book.

The Publisher will provide access to the Report Links that back up this book and will keep these Report Links up to date on **www.myreportlinks.com** for five years from the book's first publication date.

We have done our best to make sure all Internet addresses in this book were active and appropriate when we went to press. However, the author and the Publisher have no control over, and assume no liability for, the material available on those Internet sites or on other Web sites they may link to.

The usage of the MyReportLinks.com Books Web site is subject to the terms and conditions stated on the Usage Policy Statement on **www.myreportlinks.com**.

A password may be required to access the Report Links that back up this book. The password is found on the bottom of page 4 of this book.

Any comments or suggestions can be sent by e-mail to comments@myreportlinks.com or to the address on the back cover.

♻ Enslow Publishers, Inc., is committed to printing our books on recycled paper. The paper in every book contains 10% to 30% post-consumer waste (PCW). The cover board on the outside of each book contains 100% PCW. Our goal is to do our part to help young people and the environment too!

Photo Credits: AP/Wide World Photos (Elaine Thompson), p. 23; thebirdguide.com, p. 66; ExperienceWA.com, p. 100; GORP.away.com, p. 10; The Hoh River Trust, p. 17; howstuffworks.com, p. 84; The Humane Society of the United States, p. 77; © istockphoto.com: pp. 1 (inset—Natalia Bratslavsky), 6 (Hurricane Ridge) & 8 (Bill Raboin); Library of Congress, pp. 35, 38; Makah.com, p. 39; MyReportLinks.com Books, p. 4; *National Geographic,* p. 101; National Park Service/Enslow Publishers Inc., p. 5; National Park Service, pp. 7 (Mt. Olympus & Elwha River), 21, 80–81, 87, 90, 95; National Parks Conservation Association, p. 55; National Park Foundation, p. 115; National Wildlife Foundation, p. 74; NOAA, pp. 46–47, 56; Olympic Park Institute, p. 108; Oregon State University, p. 75; Photos.com, pp. 1 (background), 3, 7 (otter) & 65, 19, 26–27, 78; The Rocky Mountain Elk Foundation, p. 54; Sea World, p. 62; © shutterstock.com, pp. 6 (top banner–Olympic Mountains) & 30–31 (Sir Armstrong), 6 (Roosevelt elk) & 42–43 (Natalia Bratslavsky), 8–9 (camera), 12–13 & 14–15 (Susan Ridley), 42–43 (laptop), 61, 69 (Steffen Foerster Photography), 71 (Gregory Synstelier), 73, 80–81 (camcorder), 98–99 (Natalia Bratslavsky), 102 (Kristy Batie), 106–107 (Maxim Kazitov), 110–111 (Mike Norton), 113 (Natalia Bratslavsky); soilerosion.net, p. 82; *Timber Harvesting,* p. 86; U.S. Fish and Wildlife Service, pp. 6 (owl), 58, 93; U.S. National Snow and Ice Data Center, p. 28; University of Washington, pp. 32, 45, 48, 91, 114; visitsolduc.com, p. 104; The White House, p. 52.

Cover Photo: istockphoto.com/Natalia Bratslavsky (inset photo) and photos.com (background)

CONTENTS

MyReportLinks.com Books
Great Books, Great Links, Great for Research!

The Internet sites featured in this book can save you hours of research time. These Internet sites—we call them **"Report Links"**—are constantly changing, but we keep them up to date on our Web site.

When you see this "Approved Web Site" logo, you will know that we are directing you to a great Internet site that will help you with your research.

Give it a try! Type http://www.myreportlinks.com into your browser, click on the series title and enter the password, then click on the book title, and scroll down to the Report Links listed for this book.

The Report Links will bring you to great source documents, photographs, and illustrations. MyReportLinks.com Books save you time, feature Report Links that are kept up to date, and make report writing easier than ever! A complete listing of the Report Links can be found on pages 116–117 at the back of the book.

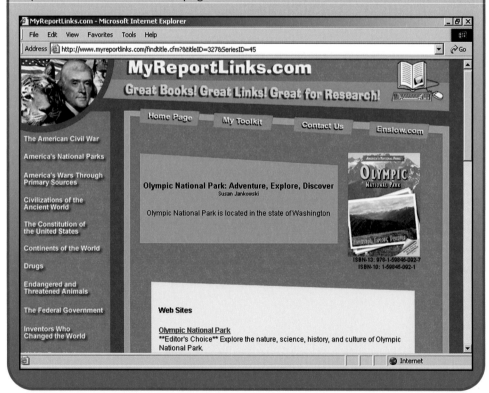

Please see "To Our Readers" on the copyright page for important information about this book, the MyReportLinks.com Web site, and the Report Links that back up this book.

Please enter ONP1460 if asked for a password.

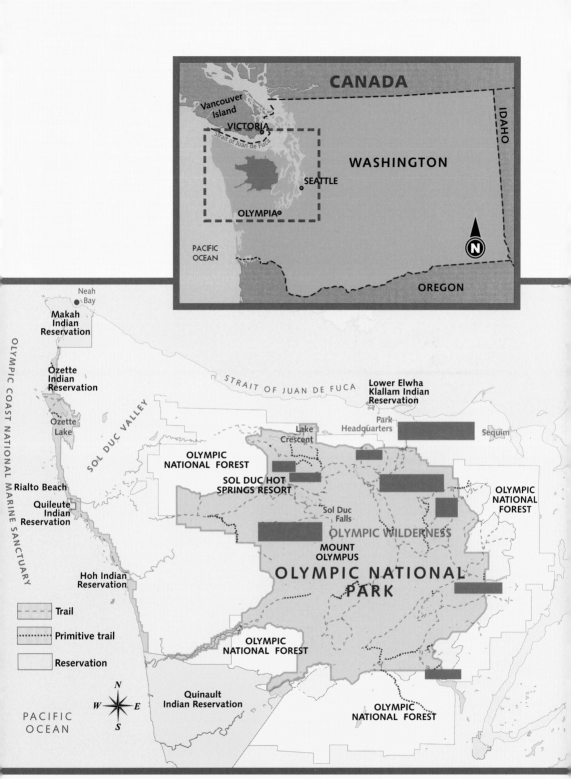

Olympic National Park, located in northwestern Washington on the Olympic peninsula, includes a stretch of Pacific coastline and borders the Strait of Juan de Fuca to the north.

The lowland forests of Olympic National Park are home to giant old-growth trees that stand nearly three hundred feet tall and are hundreds of years old. A few trees in the montane forest may be more than one thousand years old.

There are many different kinds of forests in the park, including coastal, alpine, subalpine, montane, and temperate coniferous rain forests.

The park's Hoh rain forest is ninety minutes by car from the Pacific Ocean. Although the rain forest and coastal areas of the park are very different, visitors can explore both in one day.

Olympic National Park was named for Mount Olympus, which is 7,980 feet high.

The U.S. Congress made 876,669 acres of the park's land protected wilderness in 1988. This is 95 percent of Olympic National Park's 922,651 acres.

Millions of people visit Olympic National Park each year. Park staff recorded more than 3 million visits in 2005.

The park has 611 miles of hiking trails, and seventy guided trips and hikes are available to visitors.

Some areas in the park are too dense or steep for humans to hike through.

Mount Olympus receives more than two hundred inches of precipitation per year, mostly as snow.

Ten feet of snow typically bury Hurricane Ridge, home of one of the park's popular visitors' centers, by midwinter. Deep snow and the threat of avalanches sometimes cause staff to close this center and the road leading to it.

Sixty named glaciers crown the Olympic Mountains.

Olympic National Park is a protected home for more than twenty threatened or endangered species.

⛰ Overhunting nearly wiped out animals like the Roosevelt elk and the sea otter on the Olympic Peninsula by 1900.

⛰ The park was nearly named "Elk National Park" for its resident elk herds. Roosevelt elk were named after Theodore Roosevelt, the twenty-sixth U.S. president.

⛰ The northern spotted owl is protected under the federal Endangered Species Act because of its status as a threatened species.

⛰ The Olympic marmot is a native species found only on the peninsula.

⛰ Salmon are fish that swim upstream to lay or fertilize eggs; after they spawn, they die.

⛰ Tide pools in the Olympic Coast National Marine Sanctuary are often filled with brightly colored orange starfish. They eat shellfish and sea urchins.

⛰ Today, the United States recognizes ten American Indian tribes with links to Olympic history. They are the Hoh, Jamestown S'Klallam, Elwha Klallam, Port Gamble S'Klallam, Quileute, Quinault, Skokomish, Makah, Squaxin and Suquamish tribes.

⛰ Olympic National Park's ocean coast is seventy-three miles long.

⛰ Although the park is generally too wet for forest fires to be a problem, campfires are only allowed below 3,500 feet. This rule was made to protect forests from wood gathering. There are limited firewood supplies at high elevation.

⛰ Sometimes Search and Rescue (SAR) teams are called to help injured or lost hikers or climbers in Olympic National Park. There were thirty-one SAR operations in 2005; most were due to injury.

Chapter

1

Hurricane Ridge is one of the most popular spots in the park. It offers scenic views of mountain peaks mixed with low-lying clouds.

Glaciers and Old-Growth Trees

There is a place with giant trees and vast meadows. Here, sunlight is lost in clouds that cling to mountain peaks. Rivers drop into roaring waterfalls in mists below. The water crashes onto rocks to form bubbling rapids. Then it rushes beyond Olympic National Park's glaciers, which glitter like huge diamonds on the horizon. Finally, the fresh water flows to the rolling waves of the world's greatest sea.

Mastodons and bison roamed this land thousands of years ago. Now these great beasts are gone. Yet today Olympic National Park and the national forest surrounding it are still full of life. Both the park and forest are located on a piece of Washington State that extends northwest to the Pacific Ocean. Like all peninsulas, this strip of land has water on three sides. To its north is the Strait of Juan de Fuca; east of the peninsula is Puget Sound. The park is in the center of the peninsula and on the western coast of the Pacific Ocean.

Water and sunlight are important to life in the park. There are plenty of both here. Lush valleys and forests unfold beneath the Olympic Mountains, which stand in a wide circle at the center of the park. The mountains are crowned by glaciers, or masses of snow and ice that harden over time and slowly move upon land. They sparkle in sunshine atop of the mountains.

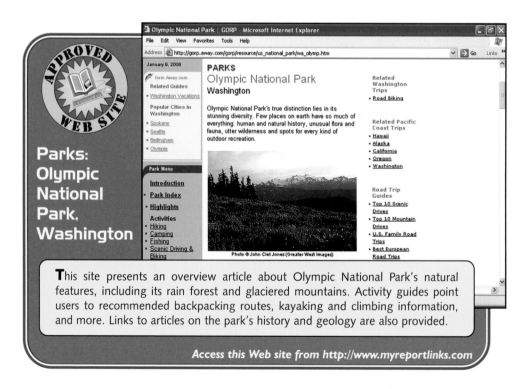

This site presents an overview article about Olympic National Park's natural features, including its rain forest and glaciered mountains. Activity guides point users to recommended backpacking routes, kayaking and climbing information, and more. Links to articles on the park's history and geology are also provided.

Access this Web site from http://www.myreportlinks.com

Storm clouds blow in from the ocean and into the mountains. For this reason, more rain falls in Olympic National Park than anywhere else in the "lower 48" states. Because there is so much water in so many different forms, life thrives here.

Early peoples lived beneath some of the very same trees people can see in the park today. Olympic National Park is famous for its forests of old-growth trees that draw visitors from across the globe every year. Some of these trees stand nearly three hundred feet high and are two centuries old. Signs are posted on some of the largest trees scientists have marked as "old growth" for tourists.

VARIETY OF LANDSCAPES

Each section of Olympic National Park features a different landscape. These include a rain forest, a mountain wilderness, and the ocean shoreline. Today, the park land is protected by the U.S. government. This means no large-scale building is allowed here. Wilderness areas receive extra protection.

The park's hiking trails and campgrounds host millions of visitors each year. It has more than six hundred miles of hiking trails. Hikers and rock climbers tackle any of a number of the Olympics' rugged or high slopes. Mount Olympus reaches nearly eight thousand feet above sea level. From such heights, the Olympic Mountains offer visitors amazing views.

Yet some areas of the park are so dense or steep that humans can only pass through them with great difficulty. Life in Olympic National Park's innermost lands can seem mysterious. American Indians in this region tell stories about supernatural creatures that they believe live in its dense forests. Some stories are about spirits who live deep in the ocean. The vast Olympic wilderness

A trail through the Hoh Rain Forest, where nearly one hundred and forty inches of rain falls each year.

has been the setting of stories and folktales for generations.

One is the famous legend of "Big Foot," which is said to be an apelike being that roams Pacific Northwest forests. People have come across large footprints they cannot explain in the Olympics, as well as at other sites across the United States. There are stories about Big Foot sightings and of

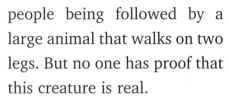

people being followed by a large animal that walks on two legs. But no one has proof that this creature is real.

However, for hikers who stray from Olympic trails, getting lost is the real danger. For this reason, park rangers tell hikers to stay on marked trails. Every spot offers scenery visitors can enjoy without having to wander into the wilderness.

The landscape bursts with color in summer. Flower blossoms cover Olympic National Park's grounds. As many as three rainbows might be spotted in the sky in a single day. In the fall, stands of big leaf maple trees cover hillsides red and gold. The warm afternoon sun and cool breeze make perfect weather for picnics and hiking.

Tourism along Olympic National Park's ocean beaches is busiest in summer, when the sun shines on the pink, orange, and yellow starfish in the park's ocean tide pools. Dozens of starfish gather in clear pools of water behind boulders on the

Starfish gather in the park's clear tide pools behind boulders on the beach.

beaches. For hours, they are protected from the strong waves of the open ocean . . . until the turn of the tide brings them out to sea again. These creatures can grow to the size of a large man's hand, or even a Frisbee. Their undersides are full of wiggling tentacles. They gather to feed on clams, mussels, and crabs along the beach.

Skiers welcome the winter season with a run on a trail covered with fresh snow. While there are snowstorms in colder months, visitors enjoy mild temperatures much of the year. The climate in Olympic National Park is connected to warm-weather cycles from the Pacific Ocean. Under partly cloudy skies, the temperature ranges from 30°F to 75°F (−1°C to 24°C), which is good for people as well as many plants and animals. But when the temperature stays just above freezing, the result is icy rain and water in all its forms. For this reason, visitors should use caution when driving on park roads.

➡ WATER: THE SOURCE OF OLYMPIC LIFE

Water in Olympic National Park is naturally "recycled." The process begins when the earth warms, which causes snow to melt. This forms streams and rivers that flow from the mountains into lakes or the ocean. These waters evaporate, and the vapor rises to form low clouds. As they rise and cool, the clouds then release water in the form of rain or snow.

The mountains keep the clouds from moving too far east. Sometimes strong gusts of wind blast off the ocean through the park. This causes low-hanging clouds to slam into the mountains. Trees snap and fall to the ground from the force of high wind. Soon rain, sleet or snow soaks the parklands below. Then the cycle begins anew.

Olympic National Park receives up to two hundred inches of rain and snow each year. Hurricane Ridge, a popular tourist spot, is often buried under ten feet of snow by midwinter. The park's Hoh Rain Forest is a ninety-minute drive from the Pacific Ocean. This rain forest receives nearly one hundred and forty inches of rain every year. It produces three times the living matter—called biomass—as in the earth's tropical rain forests.[1]

Although large prehistoric animals are long gone, a host of living things in the park benefit from the rich soil found there in the twenty-first century. The damp earth that flanks bodies of water in Olympic National Park supports all sorts of living things. Mushrooms spring to life in the shadows alongside creeks.

Striped lizards look for dry spots on logs beneath wide ferns. Large frogs leap over roots and around stumps. Snakes slip silently over mossy rocks. They prey upon salamanders in and along the streams of the park's old-growth forests. A total of

The Hoh River Trust works to conserve the lands along the Hoh River on Washington's Olympic Peninsula. Its Web site uses photos and movies to help users learn about the area's history and plan day trips to sites such as the Hoh Rain Forest or the northwest coast.

seventeen different types of amphibians (frogs, toads, newts, and salamanders) and reptiles have been seen in the park.

Orange butterflies flutter into the air until they are out of sight. Merlins, or small falcons, perch in pine trees and wait for wrens to suddenly fly out from groups of alder trees. The Olympic lowland forest is also home to northern spotted owls. They peer from old-growth trees to scan the forest floor for a mouse, young chipmunk, or a shrew.

When the rainy season ends, sunshine returns to the Olympics to boost the growth of berries on thorny branches or vines. A black bear licks black-berry juice from his paws while breathing in a salty breeze from the nearby ocean. If the bear walks a few miles downstream to the beach, he may see an orca, also known as a killer whale, rush the shore to snatch a seal. The seal cannot escape the whale's huge jaws.

Orcas live in Olympic coastal waters year-round; they feed on seals and sea lions. Dolphins, porpoises, and sharks also live in these waters. In 1988, the U.S. Congress made the Olympic coast-line a protected area for marine plants and animals.

⮕OLYMPIC LAND MAP

On a map, Olympic National Park takes up much of the center of the peninsula, as well as a long stretch of the Pacific Coast. It includes the Hoh

Rain Forest and the Olympic Mountains. The National Park Service runs it. Rules differ slightly in Olympic National Forest lands around the park. This area includes the Quinault Rain Forest south of the park. A section of ocean to the west is the Olympic Coast National Marine Sanctuary, which is run by the National Oceanographic and Atmospheric Administration (NOAA).

To the north, the border of the national park ends at the Strait of Juan de Fuca. The town of Port Angeles is along the peninsula's coast to the northeast. It is a stopover for visitors on their way to the park. To the east is Puget Sound. The cities of Seattle and Tacoma are located on Puget Sound to the south. The Kitsap Peninsula stands between

A majestic bald eagle in ▷ flight. Bald eagles are common on the Olympic Peninsula.

these cities and the national park on the Olympic Peninsula. Most people ride ferries or drive cars, or both, to get to Olympic National Park.

⇒ AMERICAN INDIANS THRIVED IN THE AREA

Humans have taken part in the Olympic food chain for centuries. The totem poles of native Northwest tribes often feature carvings of eagles, bears, salmon, orca, and other local animals. The family, or clan, feels a special connection with its chosen animal. Members of a clan often value the natural skills their chosen animal uses to survive. The carvings serve as symbols of life in the Olympics.

On the Olympic Peninsula, it is common to hear a bald eagle scream across a wide gorge to its fledgling. She will teach her offspring to fish for salmon that swim upstream to spawn. For centuries, salmon have been food for humans and animals in the Pacific Northwest.

The life cycle of a salmon involves an amazing journey. During its lifetime, a salmon travels to the ocean, then it swims back to its birthplace in a river or stream to lay or fertilize eggs. It then dies in the same location. Salmon-breeding waters make ideal hunting grounds for bald eagles and bears (as well as humans) to catch these fish.

American Indians of the Olympics still smoke salmon over fire pits as they have for hundreds of years. Native people also know which mushrooms to pick and which berries to eat. Some mushrooms and berries are toxic, and they can make people sick. But many Olympic plants are good for people. American Indians know how to use the native resources of their homeland and have passed down these skills to their children and grandchildren.

Native people thrived in the Olympics because of the bounty of life in the ocean, in the mountains, and beneath the rain-forest canopy. This canopy is a layer of branches and leaves at the tops of trees.

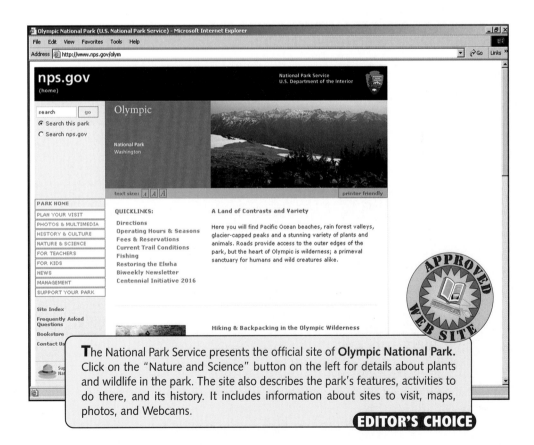

The National Park Service presents the official site of **Olympic National Park.** Click on the "Nature and Science" button on the left for details about plants and wildlife in the park. The site also describes the park's features, activities to do there, and its history. It includes information about sites to visit, maps, photos, and Webcams.

EDITOR'S CHOICE

Douglas fir, Western hemlock, Sitka spruce, and other types of evergreen trees create the forest canopy of Olympic National Park. In some places, the canopy roof is so thick that it blocks out the sky.

Cougars, bobcats, and bears crouch in the cool darkness of the canopy. Much like ancient predators, these hunters are on the prowl for food. They prey upon small mammals, such as the Olympic marmot, or large plant eaters, such as the black-tailed deer. Twenty-two threatened and endangered species live in the park, including the marmot, which is one of sixteen animals found only on the Olympic Peninsula. At least eight plants are native only to the Olympics. When a plant or animal is only found in one place, it is called "endemic."

During the fall season, a person might hear the call of a Roosevelt elk. He may be calling to warn other bulls away from his harem, or group of female elk. Or perhaps he heard a nearby mountain goat. Steller's jay birds will squawk and Douglas squirrels will scatter when they hear the sounds of elk shuffling through dry leaves with their hooves.

Native peoples of this land began hunting large mammals here twelve thousand years ago. They killed them for food and used their hides for clothing and shelter. They used cedar trees to build everything from canoes to houses. Olympic natives knew how to live well by using natural materials found on the peninsula. In modern times, they have shared what they know with historians and scientists. Today, the U. S. government works with eight American Indian tribes with links to Olympic history. They are the Hoh, the Jamestown S'Klallam, Elwha Klallam, Port Gamble S'Klallam, Quileute, Quinault, Skokomish, and Makah tribes.

Modern American Indians put their wood carvings on display for park visitors. They perform traditional dances and hold on to their old ways. Today, boats made from tree bark still carry

▽ *Makah Indians paddling away from the rising sun as they head from Neah Bay toward the Pacific Ocean. This photo was taken on a practice run for the tribe's 1999 whale hunt.*

Makah people through tide pools as they pull in fishnets or crab pots. The Makah know how to ride the ocean waves.

The tribe holds a special gray whale hunt each year. They use whaling canoes that typically carry eight people. Some animal-rights groups are against this hunt and news reporters have covered their protests. But the Makah and other tribes want to keep their rights to fish and hunt on park-lands. So far, U.S. courts have sided with the Makah and have supported the yearly whale hunt.

In the twenty-first century, American Indians still feast in community longhouses and tell stories of animals and adventure. They gather at pot-latches, or ceremonial feasts, to remember the past and talk about the future. They wear colorful costumes that reflect life among ancient trees and glittering glaciers of the Olympics.

⊜ NATURE'S FURY

Nature is an unpredictable force that may cause destruction in the Olympics. There can be avalanches of snow, an earthquake, or even an oncoming tidal wave caused by an earthquake on the other side of the planet. If this happens people must move to high ground. Although rare, these natural events are real dangers in or near Olympic National Park.

In addition, forest fires threaten life in the park. For this reason, campfires are not allowed during the summer dry season. Campfires are only allowed below 3,500 feet in the park's wilderness backcountry.[2] In fact, "burn bans" are common throughout the Pacific Northwest in summer months to prevent fires.

There are volcanoes south and east of the park. The nearby glacial Cascade Mountain Range stretches from the states of Oregon and Washington to British Columbia, Canada. The famous Mount St. Helens volcano that erupted in 1980 is part of the Cascades. It is still active, and many scientists say it could erupt again at any time. Mount Rainier, another huge, active Cascade volcano, is approximately three hours southeast of Olympic National Park.

The snowy peaks of the Olympic Mountains rise up from the green peninsula. On clear days, people in cities like Seattle can see them. Ferries carry people across Puget Sound to the outskirts of the park. From the top deck of a ferry, passengers watch the city skyline fade as they begin their journey into the Olympic wilderness.

Chapter

2

The glacier and snow-topped Olympic Mountains tower over a nearby meadow.

A Moving Peninsula

The Olympic Mountains were formed about 35 million years ago when a plate that was part of the Pacific Ocean seafloor slid beneath the landmass of the North American continent. The force of the impact with the mainland then pushed it upward into the shape of a dome. For centuries, wind, rain, and storms carved the dome into a jumble of landforms that became the Olympic Mountains. In the years that followed, glaciers formed atop of these mountains during periods of cold temperatures.[1]

Today, scientists track the movements of glaciers to learn about the earth's climate changes. Layers of ice hold clues about Earth's history. According to scientists, the last Ice Age likely began more than 1.5 to 2 million years ago and ended about ten thousand years ago. Some scientists disagree over its exact beginning and end dates.

Glaciers form when snowflakes fall in the same spot and do not melt for many years. They bond together to form a sheet of ice that slowly grows to become a glacier. The weight of the snow on the top layer of a glacier presses down on its bottom layers to make one solid mass. This process can take tens, hundreds, or even thousands of years. Sometimes the ice mass becomes so dense it absorbs all of the colors of the light spectrum but blue. This gives the glacier a beautiful blue color.

When the glacier becomes thick enough, it begins to move as one big ice mass. According to scientists at the U. S. Geological Survey, the thickness of the ice of a glacier is about half the width of its surface. Large glaciers can measure about 1,500 meters—or nearly a mile—thick. A heavy glacier sliding downhill can carve out the side of a

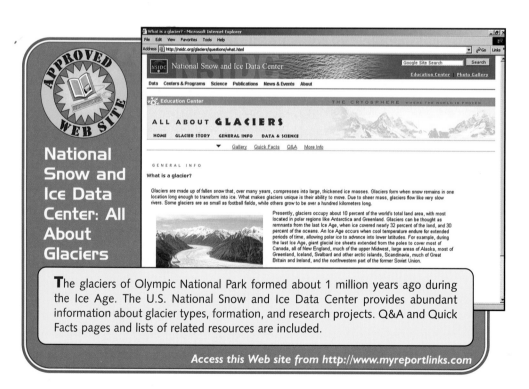

National Snow and Ice Data Center: All About Glaciers

The glaciers of Olympic National Park formed about 1 million years ago during the Ice Age. The U.S. National Snow and Ice Data Center provides abundant information about glacier types, formation, and research projects. Q&A and Quick Facts pages and lists of related resources are included.

Access this Web site from http://www.myreportlinks.com

mountain or even create a valley when it crashes down on the land below. Sometimes the flow of a glacier picks up speed and changes the landscape within a few years or even within months.[2]

More than 260 glaciers crown the Olympic Mountains today. They cover about ten square miles at the top of Mount Olympus, the tallest peak in the park. One of these is named the Blue Glacier for its color. There are sixty named glaciers in Olympic National Park in the twenty-first century. [3]

⊜ Uncovering Ancient Life

Early humans shared the Olympic Peninsula with large animals and plant species that have since died out. Using spears made from wood or stone, they hunted woolly mammoths, elk with twelve-foot-wide antlers, and bison. They had to fight off large cats and wolves to catch hoofed animals and small mammals. These predators hunted for the same prey as ancient people on Olympic parklands.[4]

A Washington farmer digging a pond near Olympic National Park found the bones of a mastodon in 1977. A broken piece of antler or bone shaped like a spear point was stuck in the skeleton's rib cage. Scientists think these bones are twelve thousand years old. This is some of the earliest proof of human hunters in the area.[5]

During a warm summer in 1993, snow melted on a bank near Olympic National Park's Hurricane

Ridge. Underneath the melting snow was a very old object. A family from Florida found it on the ground during a hike. Scientists say it was from a basket woven by someone who lived 2,900 years ago.

Researchers who study early peoples of the Pacific Northwest worked to understand what the discovery of this basket piece could mean. It could be a clue about the lives of the early peoples who traveled across North America. The American Indians in the Olympics have told stories of mountain travel for generations.

After decades of research, many scientists think the first Americans were able to cross a land bridge from northeast Asia to Alaska when ice sheets retreated in this part of the world. Early

Many glaciers top the peaks of the Olympic Mountains. The Pacific Ocean is about thirty-five miles west of the mountains.

travelers were able to journey south from Alaska and then move on to the Olympic Peninsula.[6]

Early peoples were hunters, gatherers, warriors, and traders. When European explorers came upon the Olympic Peninsula around A.D. 1590, they found skilled native people who enjoyed plenty of food. They had learned to use natural materials from the land and ocean to make tools, clothing, and houses.

In the late 1700s, Spanish explorers landed on the Pacific Northwest coast and were met by native people. Then came James Cook, the English captain who is also famous for finding what were later named the Hawaiian Islands during his travels. He returned from the Pacific and told others in

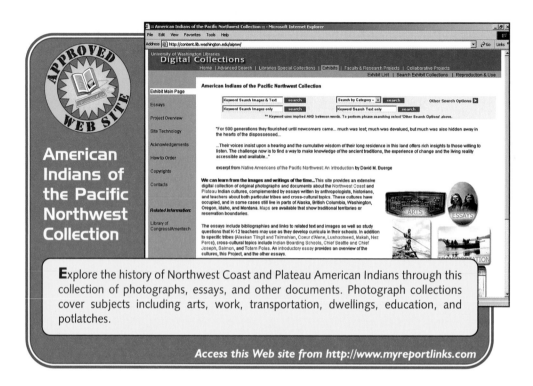

Explore the history of Northwest Coast and Plateau American Indians through this collection of photographs, essays, and other documents. Photograph collections cover subjects including arts, work, transportation, dwellings, education, and potlatches.

Access this Web site from http://www.myreportlinks.com

Europe about the thick coats of sea otters and strong skins of seals on the Olympic coast. People wanted the animal pelts to make clothing and other items. By the 1900s, overhunting of these animals had nearly wiped them out.

Before European explorers arrived, American Indians on the Olympic Peninsula were living in large villages. They did not move around to follow the buffalo and bison herds like some native tribes to the east. There was no need to leave. They could rely on salmon and other sources of food in the Olympics.

Unlike American Indian tribes of the Midwest and East Coast of the United States, native peoples of the Pacific Northwest were *not* forced to leave their homelands under the Indian Removal Act of 1830. This law was signed by President Andrew Jackson. It forced American Indians throughout the eastern half of the United States to move to reservations in Oklahoma so that white settlers could use the land. The Pacific Northwest region had not reached statehood yet, so the American Indians living there were not affected by this ruling.

➡ THREATS TO A WAY OF LIFE

At that time, much of the Pacific Northwest was unexplored. Tribes in this area are different from many other American Indian tribes in that they have kept at least parts of their homelands in the twenty-first century. Still, they struggled against white settlers, as well as other native peoples, to keep their way of life and tribal lands. European explorers wanted to hunt local animals to sell overseas. The result was overhunting that resulted in smaller numbers of these animals. The explorers also carried diseases such as smallpox and measles that were new to the native peoples. Many American Indians died from these diseases.

Olympic tribes both traded and fought with Europeans and one another. Sometimes women and children of a losing tribe were captured and forced to become slaves. American Indians fought wars over land and natural resources.[7]

→ COASTAL PEOPLE

The Salish peoples lived along the coasts of the Olympic Peninsula. Newer tribes of Salish people share a common history and language. The Klallam people on the southern shores of the Strait of Juan de Fuca were mighty warriors and good traders. In modern English, their name would mean "Strong People," or "Mighty Tribe."[8] The Klallams traded sealskins and whale oil for blankets and other goods. Tribes east of the Cascade Mountain range, such as the Yakama, traded horses for coastal treasures, such as strings of clamshells made by the Klallams.

Spanish explorer Manuel Quimper was the first European on record to meet the Klallams in their Dungeness Bay homelands on the northeast peninsula in 1790. The tribe rejected the U.S. Treaty of Point-No-Point in 1855, which would have them move to the Skokomish Reservation south of the Hood Canal. Tribal leaders would not sign this treaty at first. Their reasons included the soil on land there was different than their own, and the land was located near other tribes.[9]

Then in the late 1930s, the U.S. government set aside more than a thousand acres for the Klallams. They divided this land among three groups within their larger tribe. Today, more than 650 tribal members live on the Elwha Klallam reservation, located ten miles from the town of Port Angeles. The reservation was established in 1960.

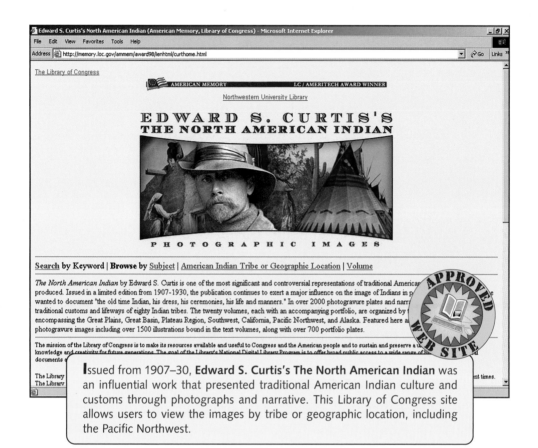

Issued from 1907–30, **Edward S. Curtis's The North American Indian** was an influential work that presented traditional American Indian culture and customs through photographs and narrative. This Library of Congress site allows users to view the images by tribe or geographic location, including the Pacific Northwest.

South of the Elwha Klallam reservation is the home of the Skokomish people, a tribe known for its skillful basket makers and wood-carvers. They traded items like these for food and clothing. Young tribal members learned their craft from skilled elders. One lesson for these young artists was to have their teacher carve one side of a totem pole; the student copied the carving on the other side. The name Skokomish means "Big River People." This tribe now lives on about eight miles of land along a river of the same name. Today, wood-carvers from these tribes are viewed as masters of such Pacific Northwest crafts.

American Indians who lived west of the Klallams and Skokomish made the coastline of the Pacific Ocean their home. Today, the Quinault Indian Reservation spans nearly two hundred thousand acres on the ocean's shores. It is home to families whose backgrounds include seven different coastal tribes: Quinault, Queet, Chinook, Cowlitz, Chehalis, Hoh, and the Quileute. Like many other American Indian tribes, their stories are about nature. Lessons about native culture come in the form of stories, teachings, and songs.

A Cedar Canoe Tradition

The Salish and Makah were among the early peoples who carved cedar trees to make canoes.[10] They had special ways of bringing down the trees. They learned how to mold the sturdy, light cedar bark into the right shape. Sometimes these longboats carried dozens of people.

In 1989, the Quileutes paddled two fifty-six-foot-long canoes one hundred and seventy miles from La Push to Seattle to celebrate their ancient bond with the Washington coast. They used this event to remind people of their special connection to the land and sea. Since then, the canoe paddle has become a major annual event for many tribes in the area.

North of the Quinault Reservation is the Hoh Indian Reservation. Olympic National Park's Hoh Rain Forest is named for this tribe. Tribal elders have helped the Hoh keep their skills as fishermen in the present day. They have created the Hoh Tribal Fisheries Program. Today, some Olympic tribes have fishing programs. They raise fish and also keep watch on wild fish.

→ THE MAKAH TRIBE

The most northwestern tip of the United States is home to the Makah tribe. This strip of land is flanked by water on three sides. Scientists have proof that the Makah have lived in this location for at least four thousand years. The Makah, however, say they have lived here much longer.

Unlike the other coastal tribes, the Makah are related to the Nootka people who live to their north on Vancouver Island, which is now part of Canada. Historians believe the two tribes may have been united in the past. Their language is tied to their roots. The Makah call themselves Kwih-ditch-chuh-ahtx (Kwee-Dich-cha-aht), which in English means "People who live by the rocks and seagulls." The Klallam tribe calls them "People of the Cape."

The Makah use harpoons to hunt seals and sea lions and also whales. They know how to make rope and fishing line from seaweed and kelp. Like other coastal people, they also know how to split

▲ *This early twentieth-century photo shows Makah whalers with their catch from Neah Bay.*

cedar trees to build canoes. In the past, the Makah and Nootka fought with the Quileute, Klallam, and other tribes.

The Makah tribe protected their whaling rights in the Treaty of Neah Bay with the U.S. government in 1855. Neah Bay is at the northwest tip of the peninsula. A half century later, the tribe stopped hunting in order to save whales, because their numbers had dropped. The Makah began hunting whales again in 1999 as the number of whales grew.

This hunt drew a lot of attention. News cameras followed both the Makah and animal-rights groups opposed to the hunt. Some people do not believe it is necessary to hunt whales in modern times. These protestors held up signs and shouted from the shore. But the Makah believe it is important to follow their tradition of holding a whale hunt once a year. This is one way to pass on their culture to Makah children in the future.

→ THE "SALMON PEOPLE"

Many of the Olympic coastal tribes had rules for handling salmon, which is a main source of food for them. They tell stories of "Salmon People" who

Makah.com: Home of the Makah People

The Makah nation is a prominent American Indian group that has lived in the Pacific Northwest for more than four thousand years. On its Web site, you can learn about its history, traditions, and current activities, including its controversial whale hunt.

Access this Web site from http://www.myreportlinks.com

live in the ocean. Each year, as the story goes, the salmon people turn themselves into fish, and then they swim up rivers to present themselves to native people who need them for food. However, native people say the spirits of the Salmon People return to the sea.

When handling salmon, American Indians are careful to return the bones to the water.[11] They say that if body parts are left on land, it could mean one of the Salmon People is missing a limb. This could anger the Salmon People, who might not return the next year. Across the park and peninsula, salmon are food for humans, bears, raccoons, bald eagles, and a host of other animals.

⇒OPENING A WATERY PATH

Today, many Northwest tribes remember the yearly return of the salmon with a special ceremony. It is an important holiday. In the past, tribes celebrated the first catch of a salmon. This special fish is still popular in restaurants across the United States today. The Elwha tribe was among those tribes that celebrated the first catch.

But the type of sockeye salmon found in this area died off after the Elwha Dam was built in 1913. The U.S. government will soon be removing the Elwha and Glines Canyon dams to open up a watery path for salmon. Parts of the dam, as well as the old powerhouse at Glines Canyon, will be left standing for people to view as a part of American history.[12, 13]

Modern engineers have since created water "ladders" to help salmon pass safely through dams. This may help other types of salmon survive in the future. Throughout western Washington, different groups of citizens, including American Indians, have come together to find ways to protect salmon. The fish has become an important symbol of life for the native tribes of the Olympics, as well as for others who have settled the Pacific Northwest.

Chapter 3

A Roosevelt elk grazes in a rain forest of Olympic National Park.

Roosevelt's Elk: History of the Park

From the start, the founders of Olympic National Park saw the peninsula as land set aside to protect elk. Its founders nearly named it Elk National Park at one point.[1] Two U.S. presidents with the same last name, as well as the five presidents who served between them, worked for a quarter of a century to turn the park into a reality.

The first step in making land on the Olympic Peninsula a national park began with President Theodore "Teddy" Roosevelt, for whom the Olympic elk is named. He founded the Olympic National Monument in 1909. He is also famous because the "Teddy bear," a popular children's toy, was named for him. President Franklin D. Roosevelt, his distant cousin, declared Olympic land a national park in 1938.

Elk are big grazing plant eaters that can weigh up to a thousand pounds. They are the cousins of moose and travel in large herds. They strip bark from trees and eat leaves for food.

Bulls lead herds of females and their offspring. Their necks swell when they let out a high sound called a bugle. Native people called them Wapiti, which means "white bottom" or "white rump."[2] Elk tend to be a silver brown color with white on their backsides.

Different kinds of elk covered the North American continent for centuries. But by the late 1800s, overhunting had wiped out most herds. After the turn of the twentieth century, the number of elk on the Olympic Peninsula and around the country was so low the species itself was in danger of becoming extinct.

⮕ "ROUGH RIDER" AND CONSERVATIONIST

Elk were also driven out of America's East Coast and Great Plains by the growth of cities during this period. The president at this time, Theodore Roosevelt, enjoyed hunting in the wild. He also liked horseback riding and many other things about America's West. Newspaper writers during this era called him "Rough Rider" or "cowboy" because he liked to track big game in the outdoors.[3]

In President Theodore Roosevelt's time, parts of the Pacific Northwest were still unexplored. Those who had dared to go into the rugged Olympic interior wanted the United States to use the peninsula as a nature preserve. President

Roosevelt liked the idea of setting aside land in the Olympics to protect elk. He was the twenty-sixth U.S. president, and one of the nation's first conservationists.

→PASSAGE TO PROTECTED LAND

There are many stories of Olympic exploration told by British sea captains who sailed from Europe to the Pacific Northwest coast. They named many landmarks in the region, including the famous Strait of Juan de Fuca, which borders the northern coast of the peninsula.

Greek sailor Juan de Fuca sailed through the strait in the late 1500s with a Spanish crew. Upon

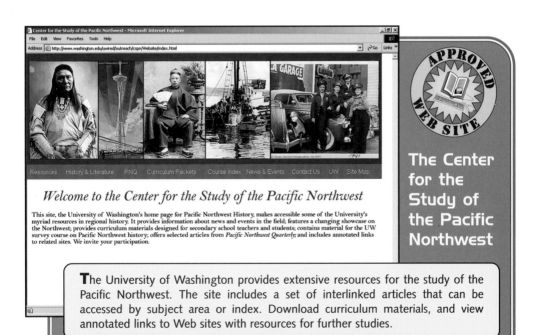

The Center for the Study of the Pacific Northwest

The University of Washington provides extensive resources for the study of the Pacific Northwest. The site includes a set of interlinked articles that can be accessed by subject area or index. Download curriculum materials, and view annotated links to Web sites with resources for further studies.

Access this Web site from http://www.myreportlinks.com

his return to Europe, he said he had discovered a passage that led from the Pacific to another ocean. No one was sure whether this story was true. Yet Juan de Fuca's story spread to Russia, France, and England. Some historians believe Spain had been sending its sea captains on secret trips to the Pacific

An aerial view of the Fuca Pillar at Cape Flattery, the furthest northwest point of the Olympic Peninsula and of the contiguous United States.

Northwest earlier than other countries in Europe. But the rich natural resources of the Northwest coast were difficult to keep secret for long. Soon many countries wanted to get into the fur trade.

James Cook also explored the Pacific Northwest in the sixteenth century and traded with

American Indians for sea otter pelts. This fur sold for good sums in China and then in Europe. On one of his visits, Cook passed Cape Flattery along the Olympic coast. This is the most northwest point on the American continent. As the story goes, Cook named it "Flattery" because the site "flattered" him into believing stories about a sea passage that stretched across America and joined two oceans.[4] (Of course, this story about the strait joining two oceans later proved to be untrue.)

In the 1800s, British captain Charles William Barkley named an ocean passage the "Strait of Juan De Fuca" on his maps. The strait joins Puget Sound and the Strait of Georgia in Canada with the Pacific Ocean. Other explorers included Captain John Meares, who sailed to the Olympic coast for furs. He named Mount Olympus after the home of the gods of ancient Greece. British Royal Navy Captain George Vancouver traveled throughout the Pacific Northwest and named many of its geographical features, including the Olympic Mountains and Mount Rainier in Washington State.[5]

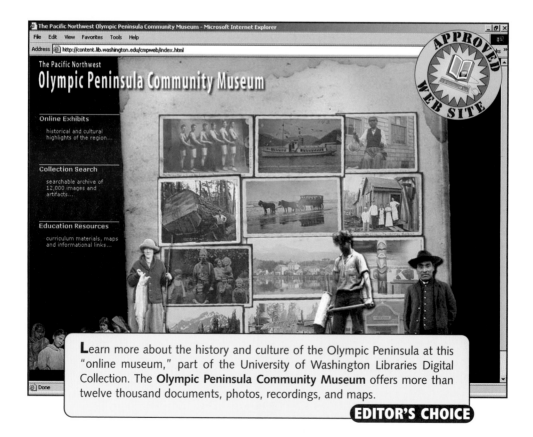

Learn more about the history and culture of the Olympic Peninsula at this "online museum," part of the University of Washington Libraries Digital Collection. The **Olympic Peninsula Community Museum** offers more than twelve thousand documents, photos, recordings, and maps.

EDITOR'S CHOICE

There are also stories of shipwrecks in this area. Survivors had no other choice but to cross the peninsula's wilderness. Native people have known the beauty of the Pacific Ocean and the Olympic forest and mountains for at least six thousand years. The truth is that no one really knows how many pairs of eyes have looked over the very edge of America to gaze at the earth's greatest ocean.

Today, much of Olympic National Park looks the same. The mighty waves of the Pacific crash into sharp rocks and scatter driftwood about. The surf booms beneath tall red cedars that cut through the blanket of fog covering the rain forest. When the weather breaks between storms, the sky becomes an ever-changing pile of clouds. This is a snapshot of the Olympic coastline. In the first half of the twentieth century, protecting this unique wilderness was on the minds of America's presidents.

NATIONAL ATTENTION

The first recorded American journey to the Olympic interior was made by U.S. Army Lieutenant Joseph P. O'Neil. He led a group of soldiers across the peninsula in the late 1800s. The men started in the town of Port Angeles, which at that time was home to only about forty people. It had a hotel, two stores, and a sawmill.[6]

It took the men about a month to travel over Hurricane Ridge. Then during their trip to the Elwha Valley, O'Neil was ordered to report to Kansas right away. The trip was cut short. He returned a few years later to lead a group of scientists on a trip from the Hood Canal to the Pacific Coast. O'Neil presented a report to members of the U.S. Congress about what he had seen. He talked about animals he saw during his travels, including healthy herds of elk, and called upon the government to help protect elk and other wildlife on the peninsula.[7]

ANSWERING A CALL FOR EXPLORERS

When Washington became a state in 1889, newspaper writers in Seattle called for brave people to explore the Olympic interior. Many people were curious about this unknown part of the Olympic Peninsula. A man named James Christie agreed to explore the Olympic interior if the newspaper company would pay for the trip. He formed a group of newspaper reporters, four dogs, and two mules. His plan was to haul fifteen-hundred pounds of supplies across the Olympics on a flat-bottomed boat named *Gertie*. He mapped out a path on the Elwha River.

But towing *Gertie* through white-water rapids and dragging her over logjams was harder than Christie thought it would be. Pulling the boat over rocks and logs tore holes in her bottom. The men finally had to leave *Gertie* behind and change their path. During the next six months, the press party traveled through harsh winter weather as it made its way through deep snow into the Quinault Valley. In May 1890, the group finally reached the Pacific Ocean. Several Olympic Mountain peaks are named for the news reporters who first explored them. This includes Mount Meany, which was named for Edmond Meany, a late *Seattle Press* editor.[8]

→ EFFORTS TO SAVE THE ELK

Meanwhile, a judge named James Wickersham was hiking in the Olympics. His party crossed paths with Lieutenant O'Neil's. They shared the view that the Olympic Peninsula should be protected land. These men saw the area as perfect for an elk reserve. Both had seen the great animals during their travels, but they also knew the number of elk was quickly declining. It was clear that the animals were in danger of dying out. For more than five thousand years, American Indians counted on the elk for the clothing and food they needed to survive. However, things had changed. Now humans would have to save the elk.

O'Neil gave members of the U.S. Congress a report about his findings on the Olympic Peninsula. He said that although the land around the

Olympics may be good for timber, the interior was too rugged for logging. Wickersham agreed with O'Neill's idea to create a nature reserve on the peninsula.[9] Their reports drew a lot of attention.

This idea won the favor of President Theodore Roosevelt. He wanted America to protect the Olympic wilderness and save animals like the elk. Writer John Muir, founder of the famous Sierra Club, also agreed with this idea. He, too, had explored parts of the Pacific Northwest.[10]

Just before leaving office in 1909, President Roosevelt created the Mount Olympus National Monument. He set aside forest lands around the mountains as breeding grounds for Olympic elk. This was one of the last things he did at the end of

The White House: Theodore Roosevelt

U.S. president Theodore (Teddy) Roosevelt founded Olympic National Monument in 1909. (President Franklin Delano Roosevelt, his distant cousin, made it a national park in 1938.) The White House presents a biography and picture of the twenty-sixth American president.

Access this Web site from http://www.myreportlinks.com

his term. President Roosevelt was one of the founders of Olympic National Park.

A scientist named C. Hart Merriam found a special kind of elk in the Olympics. He saw that Olympic elk were darker in color than their Rocky Mountain cousins east of the Cascade Mountain Range. Also, the bulls in the Olympics have longer, straighter antlers than other elk. The antlers of Rocky Mountain elk are spread farther apart. Merriam named this species "Roosevelt Elk" in honor of the first President Roosevelt.[11]

FDR PROMOTES THE PARK

President Franklin D. Roosevelt, or FDR as he was called, took office thirty years after Theodore Roosevelt. Although FDR, a Democrat, was a member of a different political party than his cousin Theodore, he often agreed with the former president. He, too, wanted to protect the elk that shared the Roosevelt name. But while FDR was in office, Americans were experiencing hard times. The Great Depression put many people out of work. During this period, feeding the nation's people must have seemed more important than protecting animals.

FDR started a plan called the New Deal. It was designed to put Americans to work clearing land for timber and farms, mostly in the West. A few years after he took office in 1933, FDR traveled to

search   GO

**Rocky Mountain
ELK FOUNDATION**

Join | Renew | Donate

Home | About Us | Conservation | Hunting | Elk Facts | News & Media | Members

Elk Facts

Fast Facts
What Are Elk
Elk In History
Elk Range
Elk Habitat
Elk Through The Seasons
How Are Elk Faring
Enjoying Elk
Managing Elk Habitat
Sharing Habitat With Elk
Elk 101
Join Us
Renew Today
Donate Now
Volunteer
Attend an Event
Shop
Support Our Partners
Link To Us

Elk Facts

Have you ever wondered how a bull elk's antlers grow, how elk stay warm in the winter or how GIS maps help wildlife biologists manage elk and their habitat? **Please click on a topic below to learn all you ever wanted to know about the wily wapiti.**

Fast Facts
What are Elk
Elk in History
Elk Range
Elk Habitat

APPROVED WEB SITE

Rocky Mountain elk differ slightly from their Roosevelt elk "cousins." Access more information about this elk's classification, habitat, range, and seasonal activity on the Web site **Rocky Mountain Elk Foundation: Elk Facts**. Learn about elk conservation and elk watching, and listen to elk bugling sounds.

the Olympics. He enjoyed the wild beauty and agreed with the first President Roosevelt that it would be best if the Olympic Peninsula was made into a national park.

FDR met with members of Congress about creating a park that could be enjoyed by people and could also protect animals like the Roosevelt elk. Five years later, the peninsula land officially became Olympic National Park. Today, it includes mountains, a rain forest, and a stretch of the Pacific Ocean.

→ COUNTING THE NUMBERS

For scientists, counting elk can be difficult when herds travel deep into dense forest areas. It is hard for scientists to record exact numbers. Some wildlife projects have involved tracking elk that have been fitted with radio transmitter collars by helicopter. Today, there are thousands of elk in Olympic National Park and on the peninsula.[12] There are now about a million wild elk across the American continent.[13]

Roosevelt elk spend springtime high in the mountains and graze in the golden valleys of the Olympics in the fall. They are often on the move through forest clearings. It is not easy to see them

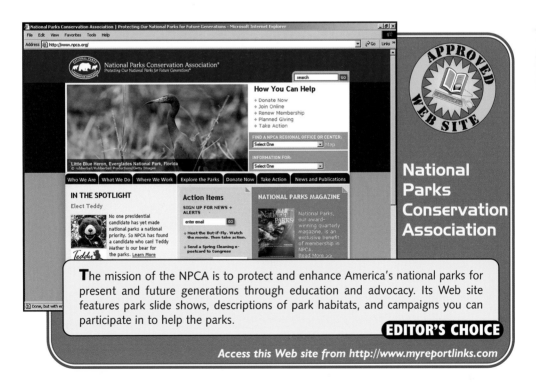

National Parks Conservation Association

The mission of the NPCA is to protect and enhance America's national parks for present and future generations through education and advocacy. Its Web site features park slide shows, descriptions of park habitats, and campaigns you can participate in to help the parks.

EDITOR'S CHOICE

Access this Web site from http://www.myreportlinks.com

when they stand still among the trees. The dark Roosevelt elk are well hidden in the Olympic Mountains and rain forests. People who know how to find elk watch for shaking brush and listen for snapping twigs to spot them.

⊜PRESERVING THE PENINSULA

During the second half of the twentieth century, more land on the Olympic Peninsula was added to the park. A stretch of the Olympic coastline became part of the park in the early 1950s. The United Nations made the park an International Biosphere Reserve in 1976, and it became a World Heritage Site in 1981.

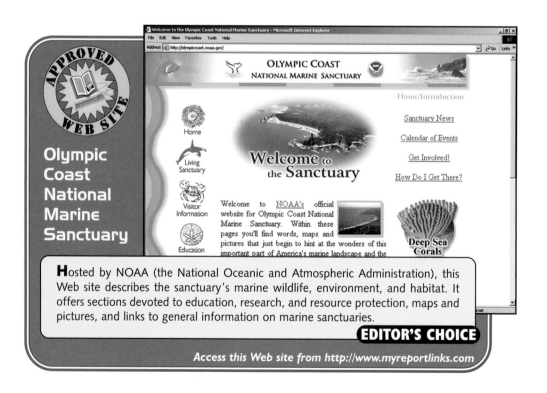

Olympic Coast National Marine Sanctuary

Hosted by NOAA (the National Oceanic and Atmospheric Administration), this Web site describes the sanctuary's marine wildlife, environment, and habitat. It offers sections devoted to education, research, and resource protection, maps and pictures, and links to general information on marine sanctuaries.

EDITOR'S CHOICE

Access this Web site from http://www.myreportlinks.com

The Olympic Coast National Marine Sanctuary was added in the mid-1990s; it stretches more than three thousand square miles into the ocean. By this time, most of the peninsula had been named a protected wilderness. This means the U.S. government limits land use here.

The Olympic Coast National Marine Sanctuary includes some of the richest shellfish and fishing grounds on the earth. It is home to twenty-nine kinds of whales, dolphins, porpoises, and other marine and land animals. The largest number of bald eagles in the United States forages for food in the sanctuary and nests on the coast in the park.

Olympic National Park is shared with American Indian tribes. Some islands off its coast are off-limits to visitors, even though native peoples can travel to them. These islands are a safe place for nesting birds, such as gulls, puffins, and auklets. Objects from early American Indians have also been found on these sites. They are important to scientists, historians, and tribal people.

Chapter 4

Spotted owls are just over a foot tall and have keen eyesight that helps them catch prey. The northern spotted owl (a subspecies) was listed as a threatened species in 1990.

Life in a Rain Cloud

Olympic National Park is home to many forms of life in every color and size. Orange salmon berry and thorny blackberry shrubs line streams splashing their way down mountains. Hillsides are flanked by red holly bushes and alpine lupines. These flowers look like pink or blue bells and hang from green stalks; some stand five feet high. On the northeast side of the peninsula, near the town of Sequim, fields of lavender flowers make stretches of land purple. Ocean breezes carry their soothing perfumelike scent.

In the rain forest, lichen covers big leaf maples and alder trees with smooth silver bark. Beneath the ocean, green kelp forests wave in the current. The kelp plant holds on to rocks and floats. It is easily uprooted by storms pounding the shoreline. In the Pacific Northwest, wide kelp leaves form a canopy much like that of a rain forest, except it is below the surface of the water.

→ CREATURES OF THE KELP FOREST AND OPEN OCEAN

Sea lions hunt octopus, squid, herring, and other small fish. They weave through underwater kelp spikes in search of food. There are different kinds of seals and sea lions that live in the Olympic Coast National Marine Sanctuary, including the Northern sea lion, or Steller sea lion as it is also called. It is a species in danger. At the turn of the twentieth century, people killed these sea lions in large numbers because it was believed they hunted the same fish that people wanted, such as pollack and salmon.

⊜STELLER SEA LION TERRITORY

These days, the sea lion's only natural enemies are sharks and orcas. About six hundred Steller sea lions spend winter months along Washington's coast. During mating season, they travel to their breeding ground, called a rookery, farther south.

Steller sea lions share the waters and rocky beaches with harbor, elephant, and fur seals, along with California sea lions, their smaller cousins. They are graceful swimmers, and they can also scramble up rocky beaches with speed. Male Steller sea lions are twice as large as females; they can grow to eleven feet long and weigh as much as two thousand pounds. Unlike females, males grow a furry mane around their broad necks. They will fight bloody battles with other bulls for territory, and will go up to two months without eating to keep their place on the rocks. Sometimes, sea lions will take over a boat dock and try to keep people out by charging at them. Then animal experts have to move the sea lions to another location.

⮕ UNIQUE BEHAVIORS

Sea lions live in large groups numbering in the hundreds. One strange behavior they have is surfacing and diving at the same time. Scientists believe that this prevents one sea lion from scaring off fish and thus ruining chances for family members to feed.

Steller sea lions are known to "play" with other sea lions, seals, and marine mammals like the

▽ A group of Steller sea lions lounge and bark on a rocky beach in the park.

Pacific white-sided dolphin and Dall's porpoise. People have spotted them tossing rocks to one another and even leaping over the backs of gray whales.[1]

Many visitors to the Washington coast have seen gray whales in spring or fall. The whales travel north to rich Alaskan feeding grounds in summer and warm Mexican waters in winter. They are a favorite among whale watchers because they are friendly to people, and have been known to come right up to boats to greet passengers.

When they surface, gray whales spout water from their blowholes atop their triangle-shaped heads. This sudden V-shaped spray can reach up

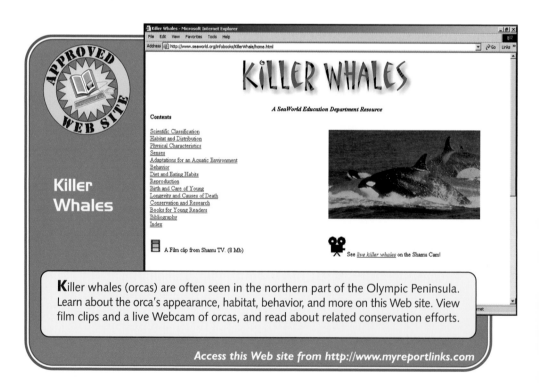

Killer Whales

Killer whales (orcas) are often seen in the northern part of the Olympic Peninsula. Learn about the orca's appearance, habitat, behavior, and more on this Web site. View film clips and a live Webcam of orcas, and read about related conservation efforts.

Access this Web site from http://www.myreportlinks.com

to fifteen feet high. Gray whales weigh as much as one thousand pounds at birth and eat enough bottom-dwelling shellfish to reach weights of forty-five tons. They can grow up to fifty feet long. They travel in small groups, and males and females are close to the same size.

Unlike other large marine animals, grays do not hunt other mammals. Now that whaling has all but stopped in the Pacific Northwest, their only natural enemies are orcas; they will kill a calf or a weakened adult whale. These waters are also a travel route for other whale species, such as the humpback, blue, fin, and sperm whales.[2]

Orcas are well known throughout Washington. Sightings are common in the Strait of Juan de Fuca across the top of the Olympic Peninsula and in busy areas of Puget Sound. This type of whale is a favorite among Northwest residents and tourists. With shiny black-and-white skin and a large mouth, the orca is often shown on hats, T-shirts, and tote bags as cute and smiling.

⊜ORCAS TOP THE FOOD CHAIN

But real orcas are at the top of the Pacific Northwest food chain. They will rush the beach to snag a seal and toss it into the air before gobbling it down. They do not prey on people and have been known to follow boats to socialize with humans. Some orcas have been trained to perform in theme parks.

Beneath the dramas created by sea lions and whales, spiny sea urchins roll with the tide. They feed on kelp until they are grabbed by animals that prey upon them. One of their enemies is the starfish; it wraps its tentacles around its prey. The thick, rich skin of starfish does not appeal to other meat eaters, however. For the most part, starfish are free to eat their fill of mussels, sea urchins, and clams in the Olympic coastal tide pools.

→Sea Otters Protected from Hunters

Sea otters live alongside sea lions and whales. They hunt shellfish beneath the kelp and float on their backs above colorful bottom-dwellers like starfish. Instead of the layer of fat called blubber that keeps other marine mammals warm, sea otters have thick fur. They may be from about two to four feet long, and the males may weigh up to about seventy-five pounds. Females are smaller.

In the past, hunters collected thousands of these small otter furs to make coats for humans. Pacific Northwest sea otters were once hunted for their fur and were nearly wiped out by 1900. A century later, sea otters are legally protected and their numbers along the Olympic coast have risen. However, in other areas, sea otters are losing their homes because of building and waste from fast-growing cities. The U.S. government lists the sea otter as a threatened species. Now it is against the law to hunt or harm these animals in any way.

Busy sea otters are fun to watch. They wrestle and dunk one another when they are not eating small sea creatures as meals. They can dive for five minutes and then return to the surface with sea urchins, crustaceans, and shellfish called bivalves.

Underneath their front limbs and along their chests are pockets of skin. Sea otters store their live cargo in these pockets, then roll on their backs. They hold stones in their front claws and pound the shells open to get to the animal inside. All four feet of the sea otter are webbed and look

Playful sea otters make their homes in Olympic's coastal waters. They are legally protected against hunting by the government.

like flippers. They are very good at paddling around shallow Olympic coastal waters. This is where they spend their lives.[3]

Along with orcas, the beaches of the Olympic coastline are dotted with tracks of coyotes, raccoons, and sometimes a cougar or black bear. Fish and marine animals are all fair game for hungry meat eaters.

IN THE CLOUDS AND ON THE GROUND

The bald eagle, America's symbol, watches life and death struggles between animals on the coast

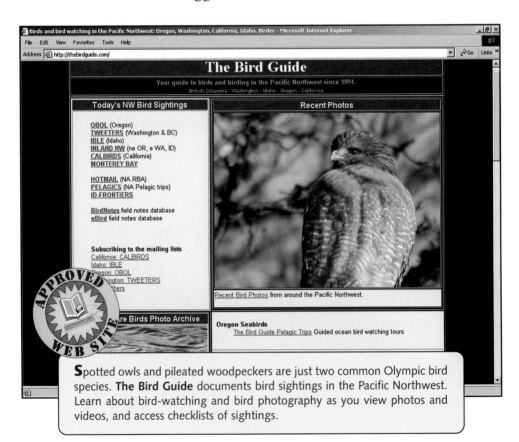

Spotted owls and pileated woodpeckers are just two common Olympic bird species. **The Bird Guide** documents bird sightings in the Pacific Northwest. Learn about bird-watching and bird photography as you view photos and videos, and access checklists of sightings.

as well as inland. It builds broad, deep nests in the Pacific Northwest forests, and it shares cliffs with the peregrine falcon and sometimes turkey vultures. The peregrine falcon is the fastest known animal on the earth. It has been clocked at nearly two hundred miles per hour in a dive through the air to catch a swallow, dove, or duck. It stakes out cliffs and most often, only one pair lives in an area.

But bald eagles perch by the hundreds along salmon-spawning beds that reach throughout the Olympics and much of western Washington State. Unlike native peoples, bald eagles leave the bodies of the salmon they've eaten along muddy stream banks. It is common to see a bald eagle in Olympic National Park, but many visitors are still thrilled when they see one.

⮕Spotted Owls With Sharp Eyesight

A spotted owl peers from inside a hollow tree and watches an eagle soar overhead. It is protecting three white eggs. Spotted owls will also live in an old red-tailed hawk or goshawk nest. They hunt northern flying squirrels, which spread their limbs and glide through the air to land on a tree branch. Spotted owls also eat rodents and insects.

These small owls are not easy to see. When they do make sounds, it is often two short hoots followed by a longer call. Just over a foot tall, spotted owls are brown with white spots and have sharp, dark eyes. This allows them to see even movements on the forest floor.

For example, the owl can spot reptiles, snakes, and frogs that live in Olympic National Park. There are also a half dozen species of salamanders, including the native Olympic torrent salamander that lives in park streams. Others include the northwestern, long-toed, and western red-backed salamanders. Cope's giant salamanders, which live only in the water, lay their eggs together in the same spot. Van Dyke's salamanders lay their eggs under rocks or decaying logs.

Salamanders do their best to avoid fish, garter snakes, and other predators. Other reptiles that live in the park include the northern alligator lizard and the rough-skinned newt. No matter how still and quiet these animals are, chances are someone in the forest, such as the owl, has noticed them.

⇒ LARGE BANANA SLUGS

But one creature the spotted owl may choose to leave alone is the banana slug. At six inches long with two wiggling tentacles on its head, the banana slug crawls along the damp Olympic lowland ground. It travels beneath plants like Scouler's ferns. These are wide plants with eight-inch fronds named for nineteenth-century botanist John Scouler. Ferns sprout on the Olympic forest floor.

Banana slugs live in Olympic National Park and throughout the Pacific Northwest. They are among the world's largest slugs. When fully stretched, they can measure a foot long! Banana slugs are easy to spot, because they are yellow with black spots.

Slugs are mollusks that move slowly across the ground with one long muscle sometimes called a

▼ Yellow banana slugs live on the damp ground of Olympic National Park's forests.

foot. They do not have a skeleton. They release a slime through their skin that helps them slide over logs and just about anything else. This coating of slime, which is actually mucus, also keeps them from drying out.

However, once another animal touches this coating, it is hard to clean off. A small mammal like a shrew, for example, may spend an hour clearing the slug slime from its mouth after eating one. This is a problem, because shrews are so active they need to eat nearly all of the time. Even though they only weigh about two ounces, shrews are always on the move; their hearts beat eight hundred times per minute![4] Raccoons have a special way of eating slugs. Before eating slugs, raccoons roll them in the dirt to bind up the slime.

MANY MUSHROOMS

Slugs eat leaves, dead plants, and animal droppings. They also like to eat mushrooms, which are fungi. Mushrooms are not alive; they are the fruit that carries the spores of a given fungus. Spores are like seeds. Slugs spread the spores as they move over the mushrooms and along the forest floor. This leads to more mushroom growth in the moist, cool shade of logs and trees.[5] There are mushrooms of different sizes and colors in Olympic National Park and across the peninsula.

With its bright red pointed head crest and white streaks along its face and underside, the pileated woodpecker can be easily spotted in the Olympic forest.

The pileated woodpecker is a bird that shares the Olympic forest with these plants and animals. At fifteen inches long, it is the Pacific Northwest's largest woodpecker. It is black with a bright red pointed head crest and white streaks along its face and underside. While it will eat berries and seeds, insects are its main meal. The beaks of these bright birds are made for pecking at insects like the Western-eyed click beetle or the giant damp-wood termite. The pileated woodpecker's favorite food is the carpenter ant, which lives inside Northwest trees.[6] From its perch high atop a rotting tree, the woodpecker can enjoy its dinner with a good view of the forest.

THE OLYMPIC MARMOT

However, the woodpecker may pass up the rough plant stinkbug that lays its eggs in a cluster on a nearby leaf. The woodpecker is probably too heavy to perch there. It will not go after the blackwitch moth or Lorquin's admiral butterfly fluttering below the canopy either. There are plenty of ants to satisfy its hunger.

Beneath the slopes of mountain meadows is the Olympic marmot. The western part of the Olympic Peninsula is the only place on earth where this kind of marmot is found. It lives in families made up of one male, two females, and their young. The marmot comes out to feed on plants at dawn and dusk.

It spends the time in between meals lying on warm rocks in the sun (except when a hunter is near).

By summer's end, the fur of the Olympic marmot changes from brown to blond. On cold days, it eats more and rests in its burrow. Full-grown Olympic marmots are eighteen to thirty-one inches long and weigh from eight to eighteen pounds. They sleep through the winter, and can lose up to one-third of their body weight during this season.[7]

The Olympic marmot, found only on the Olympic Peninsula, emerges from its burrow to feed on plants at dawn and dusk.

→TALLEST TREES OF THEIR KIND

Forestry experts have identified about a dozen trees in Olympic National Park as the tallest of their kind. Four kinds of fir and four types of hemlock trees stand at average heights of two hundred feet high or greater. A Sitka spruce near Quinault stands just below one hundred feet high. Yet this is not as tall as two cedars in this same area that are double this height. Some old-growth trees reach nearly two hundred and fifty feet high.[8]

Living on trees, rocks, and just about everywhere else are growths called lichen. When two or three organisms—usually a fungus and an alga—live closely together, they can form lichen. There

APPROVED WEB SITE

eNature.com: Olympic Marmot

The Olympic marmot is found exclusively on the peninsula for which it's named. This National Wildlife Federation-sponsored Web page discusses the species, its habitat, range, similar species, and more.

Access this Web site from http://www.myreportlinks.com

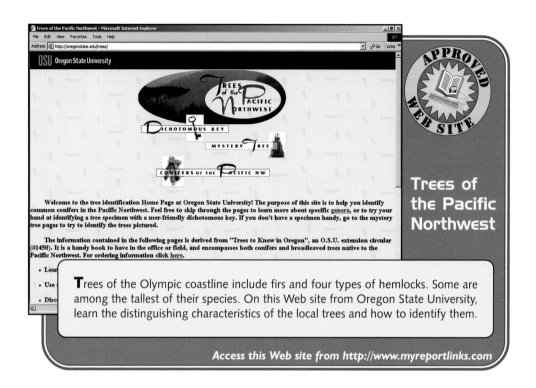

Trees of the Pacific Northwest

Trees of the Olympic coastline include firs and four types of hemlocks. Some are among the tallest of their species. On this Web site from Oregon State University, learn the distinguishing characteristics of the local trees and how to identify them.

Access this Web site from http://www.myreportlinks.com

are a thousand different kinds of lichen in the Pacific Northwest, which includes those in the forestlands of Olympic National Park. They grow up, down, and around other living things, and come in many shapes and colors. The pincushion orange lichen is found on rotting logs in the park and throughout the area. Scientists have given other Northwest lichen strange-sounding names like "freckle pelt," "pimpled kidney," and "peppered moon." [9, 10]

➲ THE "HALL OF MOSSES"

Mosses fight for forest space with lichen and mushrooms, as well as many green plants. There are many types of mosses found in the Olympics. They, too, have been given fun nicknames by scientists, such as "slender beaked" and "tangle" mosses.

The Hoh Rain Forest features a trail called the Hall of Mosses, which is a favorite among tourists. This path offers special sights that inspire artists and photographers.

Clusters of tiny flowers dot the Olympic land-scape. Along the Hoh River, visitors can enjoy seeing many small flowers, such as wood nymphs. The Hurricane Hill Trail near a main road with a similar name glows with yellow fleabane. In the highlands, from Buckhorn Pass to Marmot Pass, are other types of native plants. These include white asters, yellow daisies, Henderson's phlox, purple mountain saxifrage, gray-leaved kitten tails, Flett's violets, and different kinds of lilies and orchids.[11]

People who want to see these flowers in bloom hike on Olympic National Park trails during spring and summer. But they are not alone on the trails. Olympic National Park rangers are always on the lookout for wild animals. They keep watch to protect all living things in the park.

⊝ ALPINE ANIMALS

Sometimes visitors to the park spot mountain goats on the ledges of the Olympics. These animals stand four feet high, weigh about two hundred pounds, and traverse ledges as narrow as two inches wide. They leap among Olympic shrubs and wildflowers.

But the mountain goats are not native to the park, and this has been a problem. They tend to eat too many plants and flowers. This is called overgrazing, and it can destroy an ecosystem. A small number of mountain goats were brought here from Alaska and Canada in the 1920s, and their numbers grew to well over a thousand. When the goats clear out one kind of plant, another takes over. This may affect other animals that eat the plants, as well as the animals that eat those animals.

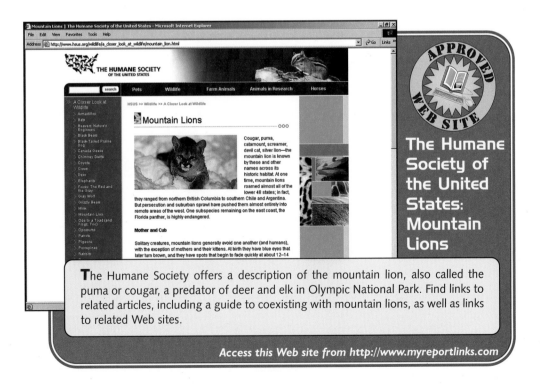

The Humane Society of the United States: Mountain Lions

The Humane Society offers a description of the mountain lion, also called the puma or cougar, a predator of deer and elk in Olympic National Park. Find links to related articles, including a guide to coexisting with mountain lions, as well as links to related Web sites.

Access this Web site from http://www.myreportlinks.com

⊜UPSETTING THE BALANCE

In this way, mountain goats have disturbed the natural balance of life in the area. Scientists have tried many methods to manage the mountain goats in the Olympics. Sometimes, they must remove or even kill them to save the Olympic alpine food chain.[12]

Many beautiful Olympic scenes include graceful animals like the black-tailed deer. These hoofed

▽ A mountain lion—the largest cat in the Pacific Northwest—shown carrying its cub.

creatures are often a welcome sight to people in the park and across the peninsula. But where there are deer or elk, there are also cougars. These large felines are also called mountain lions or sometimes pumas. They can grow up to nine feet long and weigh more than one hundred and fifty pounds. They are the largest cats in the Pacific Northwest. Cougars cannot wait to eat their kill. Their jaws and teeth are made for slicing, not chewing.

In addition to deer and elk, cougars will stalk goats, sheep, or even bobcats that cross their paths. Although it is rare, they have attacked humans or their pets in the past.

Olympic National Park rangers offer tips on what to do to avoid—or if need be, to escape—an attack by a cougar. Making some noise while hiking is a good idea. Chances are a cougar or bear, or any other animal, will try to move away from humans if it hears them coming. It is never good to surprise an animal, especially if its young are present. Running from a cougar may trigger it to stalk and then pounce. Therefore, park rangers tell people to wave their arms (to try to appear larger than the cougar), make noise, and hopefully scare it off.[13]

Chapter

5

The Elwha River is popular for fishing, rafting, and kayaking.

Dangers at Sea and on Dry Land

The Olympic Peninsula coastline, including seventy-three miles of park beaches, is always under a threat of some kind. Dangers to animals, as well as to the park itself, are both natural and man-made. For this reason, park staff and a host of weather and wildlife experts work year-round to protect parkland and its waters.

Natural events that can harm life in the park include landslides, mud slides, avalanches, earthquakes, volcanoes, fires, tidal waves, and floods. Dangers created by people include soil erosion, pollution, aging dams that create electrical power, and—along the coast—oil spills. Wild animals that cross paths with humans can be a danger to both themselves and people in the park.

→WHEN THE EARTH MOVES

Soil erosion, when the earth breaks down, is nearly always a danger in the park. This happens when there is too much wear and tear on the soil. Staff members are on guard for rock and mud slides the year round. Wind, rain, snow, storms, and foot traffic by humans and animals—all of these things can wear down the soil. It is important that visitors follow rules about staying on park trails to protect the soil and themselves. The popular Hurricane Ridge Road has been blocked by mudslides in recent years. National Park staff work with scientists and American Indian partners to protect park soil.

In winter, avalanches are a danger in the mountainous areas of the Olympics. An avalanche is a mass of snow or ice that quickly slides down a

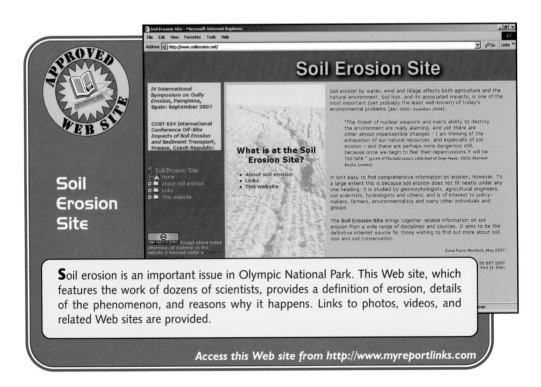

Soil erosion is an important issue in Olympic National Park. This Web site, which features the work of dozens of scientists, provides a definition of erosion, details of the phenomenon, and reasons why it happens. Links to photos, videos, and related Web sites are provided.

Access this Web site from http://www.myreportlinks.com

mountain. Often, the mass becomes larger on its way down and takes trees, rocks, and mud along with it. Sometimes experts will close down roads and cause a small avalanche on purpose to prevent a larger one from happening later on.

Earthquakes are a threat across the Pacific Northwest. The earth's crust beneath the Pacific Ocean pushes into the North American continent at the Strait of Juan de Fuca. This is called a geological subduction zone. This activity heats up the earth; when the energy builds up, it can cause an earthquake.

⇒ LARGE EARTHQUAKES NEARBY

While there have not been any large earthquakes centered at Olympic National Park in recent history, big earthquakes have happened near the park and peninsula. In the past century, there have been large earthquakes in Washington State. In 2001, Washington was struck by a quake measuring 6.8 on the Richter scale. This was the state's strongest earthquake in nearly fifty years. A magnitude 7.1 quake had struck in 1949. The tremor was felt south of the park in Seattle and in Olympia, Washington's state capitol.[1]

The damage an earthquake can cause includes knocking down trees and buildings. Afterward, it can cause avalanches, landslides, or a tidal wave, which is also called a tsunami. It is possible that

There are active volcanoes near Olympic National Park, and Mount Rainier is close by. Through photographs, diagrams, and a video, this article on the *HowStuffWorks.com* site explains the science behind volcanoes. Links to related earth science topics are included.

Access this Web site from http://www.myreportlinks.com

parklands could be affected by these kinds of natural events.

There are actives volcanoes east and south of Olympic National Park, such as Mount Baker and Glacier Peak. Mount Rainier is a giant volcano more than fourteen thousand feet in height. Should this massive volcano erupt, the impact would likely be felt by thousands of people in Washington State.

➡ FOREST FIRES AND FLOODS

Fires are a danger to nearly all of the animals and plants that live in the park's three ecosystems. There is a law in Olympic National Park that limits campfires much of the year. Most visitors do in fact follow these laws. People who ignore the fire rules or burn bans must pay fines (or worse), because one mistake can cause serious problems. After all, when underbrush is dry during the summer, a raging forest fire can start with only a spark.

Many people who live and work in Olympic National Park rake out the brush and burn it in small controlled fires. A person must obtain a permit to burn brush. Many people are finding other ways to use dried brush. For example, they form compost to mix with soil as plant food. Another thing adults can do to prevent fires is to avoid tossing lit cigarettes or cigars out of their car window or on the ground.

→ THE TIMBER WARS

Should fires get out of control, they can threaten old-growth trees. This, in turn, threatens plants and animals like the spotted owl. These small raptors rely on old trees for their homes. Whether there are enough old-growth trees to house spotted owls was a question that started an ongoing debate. People who worked in the timber industry disagreed with those who felt more needed to be done to protect the spotted owl.

In the 1980s, some people claimed the timber industry was removing too many trees and this threatened the spotted owl. Some timber industry

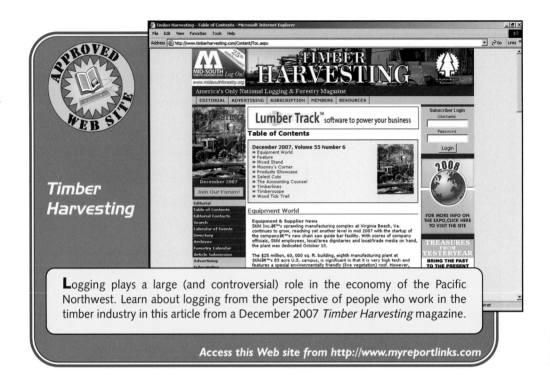

Logging plays a large (and controversial) role in the economy of the Pacific Northwest. Learn about logging from the perspective of people who work in the timber industry in this article from a December 2007 *Timber Harvesting* magazine.

Access this Web site from http://www.myreportlinks.com

workers disagreed. At times, the fight to stop forest clearing turned dangerous when people climbed trees to stop loggers from cutting them down. The debate became known as "the timber wars," and it drew national attention.

The wars ended when U.S. wildlife biologists listed the northern spotted owl (a subspecies of the spotted owl) as a threatened species in 1990 based on its falling numbers. To comply with the law, some timber operations on the Olympic Peninsula were then forced to close down. Scientists are still studying ways to help the spotted owl. The debate about how many trees the owls need continues today.[2] A new finding about the owl still makes national news.

⊕ FLOODS THREATEN PEOPLE AND ANIMALS

When the snow melts in spring and the rain soaks the ground, life in Olympic National Park is threatened by floods. This happens in the park's lowlands and on land near rivers. Floodwaters not

▽ *The severe storm water damage done to parts of Hurricane Ridge Road is shown in this photo from December 2007.*

only drown plant and some animal life in the area, but they can also wash out riverbanks and hillsides. This can result in mudslides.

In the winter of 2006–2007, heavy rains, snow, and wind from storms created flooding. Storms in the winter of 2007–2008 were also severe, resulting in washed out roads and trails, thousands of downed trees, and the destruction of other areas throughout the park. For safety reasons, park staff closed down several roads and other sections of the park. Before traveling to the park in winter or spring, it is best to call a ranger station or check the Olympic National Park Web site to make sure conditions are clear.

⊜Dangers to and From Humans

While park staff is always watching for storms, the weather in Olympic National Park can change quickly with a shift in the wind. And there are other potential dangers. An earthquake offshore can cause a tidal wave, which means people must move quickly to high ground. Signs mark the roads for people to follow if a tidal wave is coming to the Washington coast. For these reasons, planning a trip to the park or anywhere on the peninsula should include rain, snow, and emergency gear. A telephone, a radio, bottled water, protective clothing, a flashlight, and first-aid kit are important equipment for campers in the Olympic wilderness.

In addition, hikers and campers must follow rules and be careful not to stray off trails. They can prevent forest fires, keep from attracting animals with food, and call the ranger station for help if or when this is needed. It is important that visitors do their part.

⇒ PREVENTING POLLUTION

There is a saying: "Pack it in. Pack it out." This means that people should take everything they brought with them into the wilderness back out again when they leave. Many people are aware it is very important to clean up outdoors and they take care to remove their trash when they leave Olympic National Park. This keeps the park's grounds clean and helps protect wild animals and fish.

In the park, in the surrounding national forest, and beyond, pollution in streams threatens fish. Salmon travel from inland creeks and rivers out to the ocean and back again. As they move through different areas on their journey, they face many dangers, including predators and blocked waterways. People throughout the Northwest are working to save salmon and restore the waterways they depend on. The amount of control that federal, state, and local governments should have over new construction near salmon runs is an issue in Washington today.

During a storm in December 2007, the Elwha River reached record flows. This spillway at the Glines Canyon Dam is wide open to allow floodwaters to pass through it.

In the past, hydroelectric-power dams caused problems for salmon. When the Elwha Dam was built in 1913, and the Glines Canyon Dam construction followed in 1927, the number of fish in the Elwha River dropped. At the time, dams were not built with "fish ladders" that help salmon pass over the dam, so they blocked salmon travel routes. Several species of fish, including the coho, pink, chum, sockeye, and chinook salmon, were harmed by the dams. The dams also hurt the cutthroat trout, native char, and steelhead trout. In 1992, the U.S. Congress passed the Elwha River Ecosystem and Fisheries Restoration Act. Plans were delayed, and the removal of these two dams is now scheduled for 2012.[3]

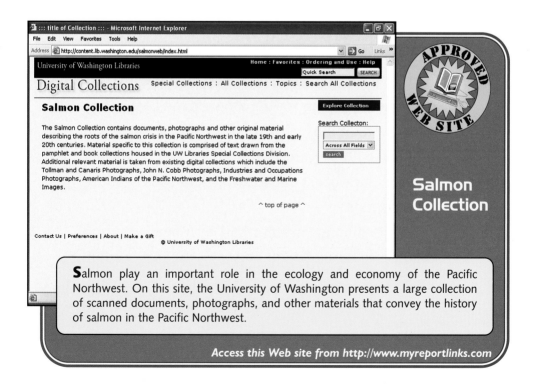

Salmon play an important role in the ecology and economy of the Pacific Northwest. On this site, the University of Washington presents a large collection of scanned documents, photographs, and other materials that convey the history of salmon in the Pacific Northwest.

Access this Web site from http://www.myreportlinks.com

Olympic American Indian tribal members work with other experts to run fish hatcheries, or fish farms, across the peninsula. The larger question of whether "farm-raised" salmon will help wild populations to survive is an ongoing one. It takes the cooperation of people in every community along a salmon run for success. Efforts on the part of people upstream can be quickly undone if a salmon run is blocked, polluted, or overfished downstream.

➔ PEOPLE AND PREDATORS

Where there are salmon, there are bears. Olympic National Park is home to black bears, which visitors see more frequently here than cougars. Bears are especially hungry when they awake from their winter's sleep in spring and also when sows, or mother bears, are nursing their cubs.

However, in the fall, bears are building up their body fat to prepare for the long winter sleep. They must eat a lot during this season, too, for they can lose up to 40 percent of their body weight during winter. Black bears can grow as large as five hundred pounds.

While humans are not part of a bear's regular diet, these animals will eagerly seek out "people food" snacks brought into the park by campers. For this reason, park staff offer special cans for food storage to visitors for a small fee.[4] If one of these cans is not available, people can hang their food from wires fastened to tree branches. Bears cannot get to the food and will likely leave the area in search of something else to eat.[5]

To avoid running into bears, people should make noise while hiking and keep food away from their tents in campgrounds. Should a bear approach, do not run but leave the area as soon as possible. Both bears and cougars will likely chase a person who runs. It is best to back away slowly from a bear to show you are going away and mean no harm. Should you cross paths with a cougar, however, remain calm and do not turn your back to it. Make noise, try to make yourself look larger (as explained in chapter 4), and try to scare it off.

Black bears are a big part of the wildlife at Olympic National Park. This U.S. Fish and Wildlife Service Web page offers a description of the black bear and its activities, history, and habitat. Threats to the species are also discussed.

Access this Web site from http://www.myreportlinks.com

Raccoons and coyotes may also try to steal food from campgrounds. Unlike bears or cougars, these animals do not travel alone. Where there is one, there is usually more. Raccoons are not easily scared off by humans. Some can carry deadly diseases like rabies. For this reason, the same food safety rules that apply to bears should be observed where raccoons are found.

It is important that visitors to the park do not litter near the water or on land. Animals may eat garbage by mistake and choke on it, become injured, or get sick and die. Plastic six-pack rings that hold beverage cans can become looped around the necks of birds like ducks, geese, or herons. For this reason, some people take the time to cut open each of the six loops when they are finished with the six-pack. Some birds and animals get tangled in, or accidentally eat, old fishing lines. People should throw away trash in sealed bags in posted areas to avoid causing harm to birds or animals.

HIKING AND CAMPING ON THE COAST

It is also important that people stay on trails and camp only on cleared campgrounds. Park rangers visit certain locations and bring news about the park. Should the worst happen and a person get lost, Search and Rescue (SAR) crews will begin looking at these locations. Once in the wilderness, it is more difficult to find someone who is lost. SAR crews save people who have strayed each year.

The key to hiking along the Olympic coastline is being aware of the schedule of the ocean tides. What appears to be a shallow beach early in the day can quickly flood into a lagoon by nightfall. Logs can be flung by incoming tides and endanger anyone or anything in their path. It is important for hikers who venture into certain beach areas to plan ahead and pay attention to the tides.

Today, people use tide charts to plan their location along the Olympic coastline. National Park staff can point visitors to safe locations, and tide charts are even available at some ranger stations.

This virtual version of the National Park Service's Junior Rangers program combines learning and fun. The site includes educational activities, a scavenger hunt, and park Webcams. Complete the activities to earn a WebRanger card, and post pictures and stories from park visits.

Access this Web site from http://www.myreportlinks.com

Some trails are also equipped with ropes to help visitors keep their footing where the ground is wet and slippery. Beach land can be made of soft or hard sand, gravel, sharp stones, driftwood, and even boulders.

⊖ OIL SPILLS IN THE OCEAN

Oil to make gasoline for cars and trucks is shipped on huge barges across the world's oceans. Oil spills caused by ships are the most difficult dangers for park rangers to control. In the end, it is up to the people who run the ships to make sure an oil spill does not occur.

A spill can occur when the oil being shipped on a tanker is somehow leaked or accidentally dumped into the water. It can wipe out intertidal animals like starfish, sea urchin, and shellfish. The spilled oil coats sea otters and birds like the marbled murrelet. An oil spill can hurt sea lions, seals, whales, and other marine mammals. It can kill many kinds of sea plants, which takes away food from many marine animals and impacts the entire coastal food chain.

Oil can coat the inside of the animals' blowholes or nostrils, which makes it difficult for them to breathe. It can also coat and weigh down feathers, which makes it hard for a bird to fly. Some animals swallow oil, or eat smaller animals coated in oil, and then become sick and even die.

Cleanup crews worked for years to repair the damage caused by a series of oil spills off the park's coast late in the last century. They washed and rewashed animals many, many times with mild soap to clean off the oil from their feathers or fur. Wildlife veterinarians often treat animals and birds after an oil spill. Sick or injured animals also need housing. Volunteers must build sometimes emergency shelters for animal care after an oil spill.

Like so many of the dangers that threaten life in Olympic National Park, the best way to protect land, people, and animals from oil spills is to prevent them from happening in the first place.

Chapter 6

A kayak at the edge of Crescent Lake, which was carved out by glaciers. Scuba diving is also popular here.

Enjoy the Ride in the Wild

The only way to travel by car around Olympic National Park is on U.S. Highway 101, which is a two-lane public road that outlines the park. Smaller roads provide short routes from this highway to popular sites. Many of these routes are named after the place of interest. Once off the road, it isn't very far to favorite park sites. It also makes it easier to find the way when traveling by car, bus, bicycle, on foot, or even on horseback.[1] The park has many miles of horse and bicycle trails for those who want to see nature up close. It is quieter on the off roads than it is on Highway 101, which is also used by drivers of logging trucks.[2]

Visitors are drawn to the park for its beauty and pristine landscapes. Many enjoy taking a Washington State ferryboat to the Olympic Peninsula and then driving a short distance to the park. There are several routes that depart from locations around Puget Sound. Ferries depart from nearby Keystone,

The Official Site of Washington State Tourism: Home Page - Microsoft Internet Explorer

File   Edit   View   Favorites   Tools   Help

Address http://www.experiencewa.com/v5/home/default.aspx   Go   Links

experiencewa.com
The Official Site of Washington State Tourism

SEARCH   GO

Home   Accommodations   Activities & Attractions   Cities   Deals   Events   Transportation   Guides & Maps

Holiday Happenings
are in full swing. Cities and
towns across the state are
bustling with excitement.

Urban Discoveries
Feel miles from civilization
with a visit to one of
Washington's many urban
green spaces – hidden
gems amidst a fast-paced
scene.

© Tomas Kaspar

Washington's tourism site, **ExperienceWA,** covers a range of attractions and activities in the state in addition to Olympic National Park. Mount Rainier, Pike Place Market, the Cascade Mountains, and the trail of Lewis and Clark are all featured here.

EDITOR'S CHOICE

Edmonds, and Bainbridge Island and carry people—and often their cars—from Seattle, Tacoma, and from Canada's British Columbia.

From the ferry, passengers can watch bald eagles fish, dolphins race, or orcas surface for a breath of air. While some people choose to stand atop the windy ferry deck, many passengers enjoy these sights from a warm seat inside the ship. Some people remain on the bottom deck in their cars. Still other people prefer to travel to the Olympic Peninsula and park by chartered boat, sailboat, or other private watercraft.

Tour buses board at ferry terminals, too. But it is best to call the bus company before your scheduled travel date to make sure there will be seats available on the bus. Sea planes, which land on water, offer an exciting way to travel to the park. There is a seaplane airline that offers flights from Seattle and other locations in western Washington to Port Angeles, which is northeast of the park.

⇒Up Close and Personal Across the Peninsula

Once on the peninsula, many people seek more personal ways to enjoy Olympic National Park. Bicyclists have their pick of rugged or smooth

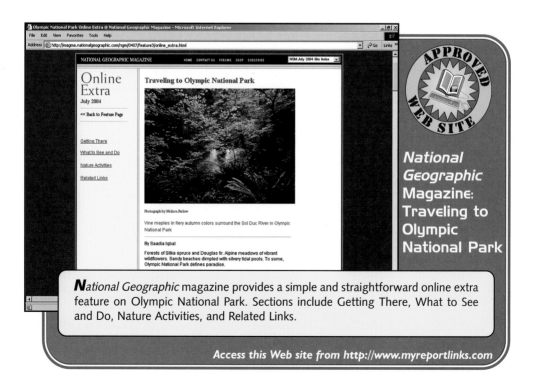

National Geographic magazine provides a simple and straightforward online extra feature on Olympic National Park. Sections include Getting There, What to See and Do, Nature Activities, and Related Links.

Access this Web site from http://www.myreportlinks.com

paths. The Spruce Railroad Trail on Lake Crescent's northern shore is popular with people who simply want to enjoy scenery while riding a bicycle along an easy trail. The Mount Mueller Trail west of Lake Crescent is more challenging. The Foothills Trail south of Port Angeles is popular with sport cyclists. There are many more trails for bicyclists across the park.

The Strait of Juan de Fuca is a favorite sea route for those who travel by sailboat. Rafting and kayaking are popular ways to enjoy the Hoh, Quileute, Sol Duc, and Elwha rivers. Sequim Bay, Port Angeles Harbor, and Clallam Bay are good spots for smaller watercraft.

▼ *A view of Sol Duc Falls in the Sol Duc Valley west of Lake Crescent.*

→ FISHING AND SCUBA DIVING

Fishing is popular on the Elwha, Bogachiel, Hoh, and Sol Duc rivers. The fresh waters of Lake Leland, Lake Aldwell, Lake Sutherland, Lake Pleasant, Lake Ozette, and others also have much to offer fishermen, who are also called anglers. Lake Crescent is twelve miles of fresh water carved out by glaciers, and is less than an hour's drive from Port Angeles. It contains two rare species of fish: the Beardslee and Crescenti trout. There are laws to limit the type and number of fish that people are allowed to catch. Some laws require people to return fish to the water after catching them—this is called "catch and release" fishing.

Charter boats carry people out from places like La Push, Neah Bay, Clallam Bay, and Sekiu for deep-sea fishing in the ocean. Hood Canal on the eastern side of the peninsula draws people who want to gather shellfish. Dungeness Harbor in the northeast is named after its most famous native animal, the Dungeness crab. Parts of the harbor are protected by the U.S. government to give fish and birds a sanctuary.

Both Lake Crescent and Lake Ozette offer scuba-diving adventures. The water in these lakes is warmer than in the ocean or Puget Sound. Because of this, many people swim in them. However, the open waters of the National Marine Sanctuary are only suitable for people with advanced diving skills.

103

Only experts can navigate their way in strong Pacific currents.

Overall, the Olympic shoreline is *not* a good place for swimming. One reason is because the water is so cold that a person cannot swim for very long without a dangerous drop in body temperature called hypothermia. Very cold water can kill a person within hours or even minutes.

Driftwood and items destroyed by storms are hurled to shore on strong ocean currents. A person can be injured or killed by a large solid object in his or her path. The cold waters in the northern Pacific have big waves that even surfers find challenging. Visitors should be careful when swimming

Sol Duc Hot Springs

Sol Duc Hot Springs Resort is affiliated with Olympic National Park. This Web site provides a good overview, including park history and FAQs, plus information on lodging and activities.

Access this Web site from http://www.myreportlinks.com

in waters throughout the park. It is best to ask park staff or tour guides to provide information about the safest places for boating, fishing, and swimming.

But visitors *can* enjoy a relaxing soak in water at the Sol Duc natural hot springs. They can settle in at the site's campground or check into a resort hotel located there. After hours of hiking, a soak in the hot springs soothes tired muscles. It is also a great way to warm up during chilly weather.[3]

⟶ VIEWS ALL AROUND

Hurricane Ridge, which offers scenic views of Olympic glaciers, Mount Olympus, and the Strait of Juan de Fuca, is named for the strong winds that occur there. One of the park's most popular visitors' centers is located on the ridge. It offers views from atop the ridge a mile above sea level. Binoculars help people get a closer look at wildlife from the ridge. Hikers and cross-country skiers often start at this site, which is less than an hour's drive from the town of Port Angeles.

In winter, cross-country skiers glide over trails opened for this season at Hurricane Ridge. There are also snowshoe trails and a downhill ski area, as well as a play area for inner tubing, sledding, and sliding in what is truly a winter wonderland.

At certain times, popular sites around the park are filled with visitors. To avoid crowds, park staff advises getting an early start in the morning.

Whether visitors travel by recreational vehicles (RVs), camp, or stay at the local lodge, there is always something to see and do in the park. Every form of travel offers unforgettable scenery. Photographers never tire of taking pictures in Olympic National Park. At times, the park's landscape can look like a living postcard.

The Staircase site has river rapids located at the North Fork of the Skokomish River. This is near the southeast corner of the park. Its white water flows too quickly for swimmers. But people come by the hundreds to watch the fast-moving waters. Few can resist snapping a photograph here.

▼ *Skiers enjoy cross-country and downhill skiing at Hurricane Ridge during the winter season.*

For visitors who like the comforts of home, resorts throughout the park offer modern activities, such as golfing, shopping, and dining at restaurants. For those who like to sleep and eat closer to nature, the park has many campgrounds.

⊜ CAMPING IS KING

Nearly all park locations have campgrounds near the site of interest. Deer Park is a remote campground located below a six-thousand-foot summit of the Blue Mountain. Just outside park boundaries, in the old-growth rain forest near Lake Quinault, three U.S. Forest Service campgrounds contain more than fifty campsites. These are located at Falls Creek, Willaby, and Gatton Creek. Some have running water, while others do not. On the coast, Kalaloch provides wide views of a vast shoreline with private campsites.

People come from all over the world to Olympic National Park to marvel at the Hoh Rain Forest. Further south, the Quinault Rain Forest also draws a lot of visitors. Once out of the car and on the walkway or trail, visitors can feel the rain forest's natural moisture on their skin and as they breathe. They can step over banana slugs, walk under branches full of hanging moss, stand under old-growth trees hundreds of feet high, and listen for the call of a spotted owl. If they get an early start, they can leave from Hoh Rain Forest by noon. Then it's time for a scenic drive to Rialto Beach to watch the sunset. This site is near the town of La Push on the ocean.

Out in the distance from Cape Flattery, north of La Push, are Cape Alava and the island of Tatoosh. The island is named for an American Indian chief and is home to a lighthouse. These areas are presently off-limits to visitors to protect birds that rest there and fossils uncovered by scientists.

Olympic Park Institute

Make your visit to Olympic National Park a learning adventure! The Olympic Park Institute is devoted to science and environmental education. Its Web site includes educational projects for before and after a park visit, and links to additional park resources.

EDITOR'S CHOICE

Access this Web site from http://www.myreportlinks.com

South of Cape Flattery is a historical museum at Ozette. This museum displays a village full of longhouses, boats, tools, clothing, and other items made by native peoples centuries ago. Near this site on the ocean is a national landmark named the Point of Arches. Here, rock formations spiral to the sky. The strange figures are among the most photographed and painted in the world. They add to the mystery of the Olympics in ancient times.

→ THE PAST BECOMES THE FUTURE

A winter storm in 1970 uncovered an early Makah village. Scientists learned that beneath the gravel and sand, longboats and longhouses had been preserved for five hundred years. The houses are large rectangle-shaped buildings made of wood. They were home to many families at the same time. The boats were sturdy and often carved with the faces of animals that served as the family, or clan, symbol. Some people call this animal symbol a totem.

Today, the Makah tribe shares its rich history with visitors. They value these objects, which were probably buried in a landslide centuries ago. The tribe built a museum for these items. Smaller objects on display include baskets and weapons. The museum reflects the Makah's past as hunters, gatherers, fishermen, artists, craftsmen, warriors, and traders.[4]

There is much to do in Olympic National Park, and many ways to learn about its different

A sunset at Second Beach in Olympic National Park.

ecosystems and rich history. Towns across the Olympic Peninsula offer information on the history of logging and sea adventures in the Northwest. American Indian reservations open the doors to their tribal centers and gift shops to welcome curious visitors. Learning about the park helps people appreciate this pristine wilderness in the present day.

MOUNTAIN, FOREST, AND SEA FESTIVALS

Each year, there are festivals that celebrate life in Olympic National Park and around the peninsula. Farmers' markets are open year-round in Port Angeles. The Wooden Boat Festival in Port Townsend is one of the most popular such events in the Pacific Northwest. It is held in late summer/early fall, and is hosted by wooden-boat builders who carry on the town's history as a seaport. Still many "land lovers" come to relax and enjoy the peaceful sight of boats floating in the harbor.

In spring, Port Townsend also hosts a rhododendron festival when flowers of the same name are in full bloom. These large blossoms of bright pink, purple, and orange are a sign that spring has arrived. Farther south, the Brinnon ShrimpFest kicks off the warm weather. In mid-July, visitors flock to the Lavender Festival in Sequim. It attracts people from all across the Pacific Northwest and Canada. Locals share their recipes for foods cooked with lavender as well as beauty items and decorations made with it.

In late summer, the other side of the peninsula is full of activity. During Makah Days, visitors can have fun watching a parade, shopping at a street fair, playing traditional tribal games, eating baked salmon, and watching tribal dances. The Clallam

Lavender blooms in the Pacific Northwest. The plant is celebrated at an annual festival in the town of Sequim.

Bay and Sekiu Fun Days festival is also held each summer. These two native fishing villages of the Olympic northern coast feature parades, cookouts, picnics, and many other fun activities. In the fall, there is the Dungeness crab and Seafood Festival. For a small fee, hungry guests eat their fill of Dungeness crab and other seafoods.

For a traditional American experience, people can spend Independence Day in the timber town of Forks. Holiday events include an old-fashioned parade, car races, horseshoe games, sack races, a frog jump, and a salmon bake.

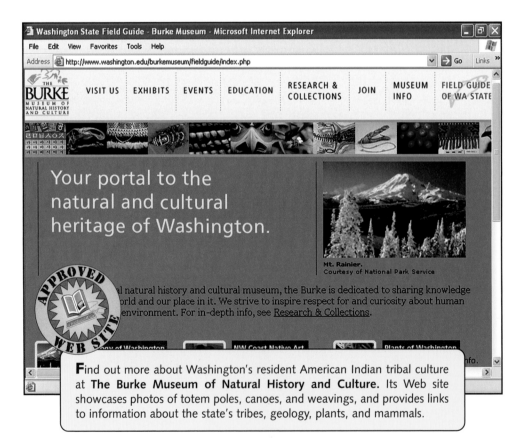

Find out more about Washington's resident American Indian tribal culture at **The Burke Museum of Natural History and Culture.** Its Web site showcases photos of totem poles, canoes, and weavings, and provides links to information about the state's tribes, geology, plants, and mammals.

The nonprofit National Park Foundation helps to maintain and promote America's national parks. On its Web site you can plan a vacation, learn about the Junior Ranger program, and read and submit "inside information" based on your own park visits.

Access this Web site from http://www.myreportlinks.com

But after the smoke from the fireworks has cleared and the celebration is over, it's back to work. Staff, scientists, road crews, rescue teams, the U.S. Coast Guard, American Indian tribal people, citizens, and visitors will keep working together to protect the park's wilderness areas. Their efforts will ensure the mountains, lowland rain forests, and ocean shores of Olympic National Park will be full of life for years to come.

Report Links

The Internet sites described below can be accessed at http://www.myreportlinks.com

▶**Olympic National Park**
Editor's Choice Explore the nature, science, history, and culture of Olympic National Park.

▶**Olympic Park Institute**
Editor's Choice Learn about the environment through hands-on activities at Olympic National Park.

▶**Olympic Coast National Marine Sanctuary**
Editor's Choice Discover the history and wildlife of the Olympic Coast marine sanctuary.

▶**Olympic Peninsula Community Museum**
Editor's Choice Explore a wealth of historical materials covering the Olympic Peninsula.

▶**National Parks Conservation Association**
Editor's Choice Read about the natural resources and habitats found in America's national parks.

▶**ExperienceWA.com**
Editor's Choice Explore the state of Washington's exciting attractions and recreational activities.

▶**American Black Bear**
Learn all about the black bear's habitat, activities, and history.

▶**American Indians of the Pacific Northwest Collection**
Explore the rich history of American Indians in the area that surrounds Olympic National Park.

▶**The Bird Guide**
Check out the bird species found in the Pacific Northwest!

▶**The Burke Museum of Natural History and Culture**
The site of Washington's oldest natural history and cultural museum.

▶**The Center for the Study of the Pacific Northwest**
Discover the history of the Pacific Northwest.

▶**Edward S. Curtis's The North American Indian**
Explore a wealth of historical images of American Indians in the Pacific Northwest.

▶**eNature.com: Olympic Marmot**
Read about a species of marmot (from the squirrel family) named for the Olympic area.

▶**Hoh River Trust**
Explore one of the last great American rivers, the Hoh.

▶**How Volcanoes Work**
Discover the earth science behind volcanoes.

Report Links

The Internet sites described below can be accessed at http://www.myreportlinks.com

▶ **The Humane Society of the United States: Mountain Lions**
Learn more about mountain lions, one of the predators found in Olympic National Park.

▶ **Killer Whales**
Learn about the life and habitat of killer whales and see a clip of Shamu, a famous orca.

▶ **Makah.com: Home of the Makah People**
Learn about the history and present-day operations of the Makah Nation.

▶ *National Geographic* **Magazine: Traveling to Olympic National Park**
Explore Olympic National Park with an informative overview from *National Geographic*.

▶ **National Park Foundation**
Read about the National Park Foundation's efforts to help our parks through volunteer service.

▶ **National Snow and Ice Data Center: All About Glaciers**
Learn the science behind glacier formation.

▶ **Parks: Olympic National Park, Washington**
Read an overview of the park and learn about the activities you can do there.

▶ **Rocky Mountain Elk Foundation: Elk Facts**
Find fun facts and serious science at this site on elks.

▶ **Salmon Collection**
Learn about the important role of salmon in the economy and ecology of the Pacific Northwest.

▶ **Soil Erosion Site**
What causes soil erosion, and why should we care? Find out at this site.

▶ **Sol Duc Hot Springs Resort**
Explore one of Olympic National Park's top attractions, Sol Duc Hot Springs.

▶ *Timber Harvesting*
Gain an understanding of logging from those who do it as a livelihood.

▶ **Trees of the Pacific Northwest**
Learn about the different types of trees found in the Pacific Northwest.

▶ **WebRangers**
Earn your Junior Ranger certification without leaving home!

▶ **The White House: Theodore Roosevelt**
Read about the U.S. president who was instrumental in the establishment of this park.

algae—Tiny green plant-like organisms that grow in water.

alpine—Mountain climate.

basalt—Volcanic rock.

biomass—Living or once-living material.

biosphere—Area of Earth's environment in which life occurs.

canopy—Thick cover from trees and their leaves at the top of a forest.

conservationist—One who works to protect nature.

contiguous—Touching or connected throughout; unbroken.

continent—One of the great landmasses, or divisions of land, on Earth.

ecosystem—An area that is made up of certain kinds of animals and plants, which create a food chain of living things.

element—In nature, the elements can mean air, water, fire.

evaporate—Water turns from liquid form to gas.

expedition—Planned trip for the purpose of exploring.

glacier—A moving mass of ice that is formed by hardened snow.

international—Worldwide; of many nations.

marine—Water dwelling; of the sea.

natural—Not made by humans; from nature.

peninsula—Stretch of land surrounded by water on three sides.

potlatch—An American Indian ceremonial feast that serves as a social occasion to mark a significant passage in life (for example, the birth of a child or a marriage).

preserve—Land that is used as a protected home for animals.

pristine—Clean and unspoiled.

resources—Source of wealth.

sanctuary—Protected land set aside for plants and animals.

spore—A simple cell body that can grow.

symbiotic—The living together in close union of two organisms.

traverse—To travel across or over.

U.S. Congress—The legislative branch of the U.S. federal government.

Chapter 1. Glaciers and Old-Growth Trees

1. National Park Service, "Olympic National Park—Lowland Forests," July 26, 2006, <http://www.nps.gov/olym/naturescience/lowland-forests.htm> (July 12, 2007).

2. National Park Service, "Olympic National Park and Olympic National Forest Lift Fire Restrictions," September 22, 2006, <http://www.nps.gov/olym/parknews/fire-restrictions-lifted.htm> (November 13, 2007).

Chapter 2. A Moving Peninsula

1. American Park Network, "Olympic Geology: Creation of the Olympics," 2001, <http://www.americanparknetwork.com/parkinfo/ol/geology/index.html> (June 15, 2007).

2. USGS, "Common Questions and Myths about Glaciers," January 2007, <http://ak.water.usgs.gov/glaciology/FAQ.htm> (June 15, 2007).

3. Olympic National Park Service Staff, "Glaciers in the Olympic National Park," *Olympic National Park,* n.d., <http://www.sequim.com/park/glaciers.html> (June 15, 2007).

4. Museum Victoria Australia, "Prehistoric Life/ North America, n.d., <http://www.museum.vic.gov.au/prehistoric/mammals/america.html> (July 8, 2007).

5. The Archaeological Conservancy, "Some of Our Western Preserves," *Manis Mastodon Site,* n.d., <http://www.americanarchaeology.com/western1.html> (July 1, 2007).

6. Microsoft Corp., "VI: First Americans," 1993–2007, <http://encarta.msn.com/encyclopedia_701509129_2/First_Americans.html> (July 17, 2007).

7. Jay Miller, "Alaskan Tlingit and Tsimshian," *University of Washington Libraries Digital Collections,* n.d., <http://content.lib.washington.edu/aipnw /miller1.html> (June 15, 2007).

8. "Unearthing Tse-whit-Zen, Part 2: Spirit of Pestilence," *The Seattle Times,* May 22–25, 2005, <http://seattletimes.nwsource.com/html/localnews/ klallamday2.html> (June 15, 2007).

9. HistoryLink Staff, "Treaty of Point No Point, 1855," January 15, 2004, <http://www.historylink .org/essays/output.cfm?file_id=5637> (July 12, 2007).

10. Kit Oldham, "Clallam County—Thumbnail History," December 27, 2005, <http://www.historylink .org/essays/output.cfm?file_id=7576> (July 1, 2007).

11. *Native-Online.com,* "Salmon," n.d., <http:// www.nativeonline.com/legends.html#SALMON> (June 15, 2007).

12. U.S. Department of Interior, Bureau of Reclamation, Pacific Northwest Region, Boise Idaho, "Elwha River Restoration Project, Washington: Elwha Technical Series, PN-95-7," May 1996, <www.nps .gov/archive/olym/elwha/reclamation/removal.htm> (July 18, 2007).

13. National Park Service, "Elwha Ecosystem Restoration," *Olympic National Park,* October 9, 2007, <http://www.nps.gov/olym/naturescience/elwha-ecosystem-restoration.htm> (July 18, 2007).

Chapter 3. Roosevelt's Elk: History of the Park

1. National Park Service, "Terrestrial Mammal Species List," *Olympic National Park,* July 25, 2006, <http://www.nps.gov/olym/naturescience/mammal-species-list.htm> (November 13, 2007).

2. Answers.com, "Word Origins: Wapiti," n.d., <http://www.answers.com/topic/wapiti> (June 15, 2007).

3. Sarah Watts, *Rough Rider in the White House:*

Theodore Roosevelt and the Politics of Desire (Chicago: University of Chicago Press, 2003), excerpt accessed online at: <http://www.press.uchicago.edu/Misc /Chicago/876071.html> (July 1, 2007).

4. National Marine Sanctuaries, "Olympic Coast: National Marine Sanctuary: History," July 30, 2004, <http://olympiccoast.noaa.gov/living/history_and_ culture/history/welcome.html> (July 1, 2007).

5. National Park Service, "Discover Olympic: Euro-American History from 1592 to 1981," *Olympic National Park,* n.d., <http://www.nps.gov/archive/ olym/edhis.htm> (June 15, 2007).

6. John William Uhler, "History," *Olympic National Park Information Page,* 1995–2007, <http://www .olympic.national-park.com/info.htm#his> (June 1, 2007).

7. Ibid.

8. Ibid.

9. "Parks: Olympic National Park/History," 1999–2007, <http://gorp.away.com/gorp/resource /us_national_park/wa/his_oly.htm> (May 15, 2007).

10. Paula Laubner Lechter, "The Goblins and Dragons of the Pacific Northwest," *Apogee Photo Magazine,* 1995–2004, <http://www.apogeephoto .com/mag4-6/mag4-6Lechten.shtml> (May 25, 2007).

11. Greg Tollefson, "Roosevelt Elk," *Discovering Lewis & Clark,* 1998, <http://www.lewis-clark.org /content/content-article.asp?ArticleID=358> (July 1, 2007).

12. Russell Link, "Living With Wildlife: Elk," *Washington Department of Fish and Wildlife,* 2007, <http://wdfw.wa.gov/wlm/living/elk.htm#problems> (July 20, 2007).

13. Tamara Eder, *Mammals of Washington and Oregon,* (Renton, Wash.: Lone Pine Publishing, 2002), pp. 40–41.

Chapter 4. Life in a Rain Cloud

1. Tamara Eder, *Mammals of Washington and Oregon,* (Renton, Wash.: Lone Pine Publishing, 2002), pp. 152–153.

2. Ibid., pp. 66–67.

3. Ibid., pp. 130–131.

4. Ruth Kirk with Jerry Franklin, *The Olympic Rain Forest: An Ecological Web,* (Seattle: University of Washington Press, 1992), pp. 71–72.

5. Donna Hill, "Banana Slug," 1997, <www .naturepark.com/bslug.htm> (July 18, 2007).

6. Eric Day, "Carpenter Ant," *Virginia Cooperative Extension,* June 1999, <http://www.ext.vt.edu /departments/entomology/factsheets/carpants.html> (July 20, 2007).

7. Eder, pp. 258–259.

8. National Park Service, "Temperate Rain Forests," *Olympic National Park,* August 2007, <http://www.nps.gov/olym/naturescience/temperate -rain-forests.htm> (July 8, 2007).

9. Jim Pojar and Andy Mackinnon, *Plants of the Pacific Northwest,* (Renton, Wash.: Lone Pine Publishing, 1994), pp. 488–492.

10. "Common Brophyte and Lichen Species of the Northwest Forest," n.d., <http://www.borealforest. com.org/lichens/linchen8.htm> (July 18, 2007).

11. Ira Spring and Art Kruckeberg, *Best Wildflower Hikes* (Seattle: The Mountaineers Books, 2004), pp. 36–55.

12. Tim McNulty, *Olympic National Park: A Natural History* (Boston: Houghton Mifflin Company, 1996; 2003 Tim McNulty), pp. 57–58.

13. National Park Service, "Wilderness Safety," *Olympic National Park,* June 13, 2007, <http://www .nps.gov/olym/planyourvisit/wilderness-safety.htm> (July 15, 2007).

Chapter 5. Dangers at Sea and on Dry Land

1. "Northwest US sits in quake zone," *BBC News,* March 1, 2001, <http://news.bbc.co.uk/1/hi/sci/tech /1196926.stm> (July 10, 2007).

2. "Northern spotted owl's decline revives old concerns," *The Christian Science Monitor,* June 27, 2007, <http://news.yahoo.com/s/csm/20070627/ts_csm/ aowl> (July 19, 2007).

3. Lynda V. Mapes, "Dam's removal will have to wait," *The Seattle Times,* April 24, 2007, <http:// seattletimes.nwsource.com/html/localnews/2003678478 _elwha24m.html> (July 12, 2007).

4. "Wilderness Safety," *National Park Service,* June 13, 2007, <http://www.nps.gov/olym/planyourvisit /wilderness-safety.htm> (July 15, 2007).

5. Ibid.

Chapter 6. Enjoy the Ride in the Wild

1. "Discover and Explore the Pathways to the Pacific," *Olympic Discovery Trail,* April 2006, <http://www.peninsulatrailcoalition.com/PlanningTrip .htm> (July 8, 2007).

2. Lawrence W. Cheek, "Washington: Olympic National Park," June 22, 2006, <http://www.msnbc .msn.com/id/12532271/> (July 8, 2007).

3. *Sol Duc Hot Springs Resort,* n.d., <http://www .visitsolduc.com/> (July 15, 2007).

4. The Makah Nation on Washington's Olympic Peninsula, n.d., <http://www.northolympic.com/ makah/> (July 1, 2007).

Collard, Sneed B., III. *In The Rain Forest Canopy*. New York: Marshall Cavendish Benchmark, 2006.

Johnson, Michael and Duncan Clarke. *Native Tribes of the Great Basin and Plateau*. Milwaukee: World Almanac Library, 2004.

Kraft, Betsy Harvey. *Theodore Roosevelt: Champion of the American Spirit*. New York: Clarion Books, 2003.

Leach, Nicky. *Olympic National Park: A Timeless Refuge*. Mariposa, Calif.: Sierra Press, 2007.

McNulty, Tim. *Olympic National Park: A Natural History*. Seattle: University of Washington Press, 2003.

Nelson, Sharlene and Ted Nelson. *The Makah*. New York: Franklin Watts, 2003.

Novey, Levi. *Olympic National Park Pocket Guide*. Guilford, Conn.: Globe Pequot Press, 2008.

Robson, Gary D. and Robert Rath. *Who Pooped in the Park? Olympic National Park*. Helena, Mont.: Farcountry Press, 2006.

Sedam, Michael T. *Olympic Peninsula: The Grace and Grandeur*. Osceola, Wisc.: Voyageur Press, 2002.

Trueit, Trudi Strain. *Volcanoes*. New York: Franklin Watts, 2003.

WITHDRAWN